Variability in Perspectives on Current Issues in Social Sciences

WARSAW STUDIES IN PHILOSOPHY AND SOCIAL SCIENCES

Edited by
Tadeusz Szawiel and Jakub Kloc-Konkołowicz

VOLUME 11

PETER LANG

Daniel Bešina (ed.)

Variability in Perspectives on Current Issues in Social Sciences

PETER LANG

Bibliographic Information published by the Deutsche Nationalbibliothek
The Deutsche Nationalbibliothek lists this publication in the Deutsche
Nationalbibliografie; detailed bibliographic data is available in the
internet at http://dnb.d-nb.de.

Library of Congress Cataloging-in-Publication Data
A CIP catalog record for this book has been applied for at the
Library of Congress.

Publication of this book was financially supported by Constantine the Philosopher
University in Nitra.

Cover illustration: © Shutterstock.com/april70

Printed by CPI books GmbH, Leck

ISSN 2196-0143 • ISBN 978-3-631-80282-3 (Print)
E-ISBN 978-3-631-80611-1 (E-PDF) • E-ISBN 978-3-631-80612-8 (EPUB)
E-ISBN 978-3-631-80613-5 (MOBI) • DOI 10.3726/b16317

© Peter Lang GmbH
Internationaler Verlag der Wissenschaften
Berlin 2020

This publication has been peer reviewed.

www.peterlang.com

Table of Contents

Introduction

Social and human sciences are currently in a special position. On the one hand, they are subject to frequent doubts and mistrust while on the other hand, there is a view that the 21st century will be a century of social and human sciences, addressing their importance in solving key cultural and social issues of humanity. These disciplines, by means of their own research methods, acquire information that helps them to understand the world and the place of man in it; they make a significant contribution to the formation of cultural memory or represent a means of orientation in the varied pictures of the world.

In our social cognitive and evaluation connection to reality we can observe the decreasing interest in human and social sciences. However, the rejection of the importance of human sciences is based on a fundamental misconception of facts. Society's education and culture is a prerequisite for the economic level of each country. Innovation is not only a matter of technical importance, it is equally important to understand human cultural behavior in the broadest possible context.

The publication contains a number of variable views on selected topics from social, human and historical sciences that demonstrate the relevance of the research in the area under consideration. Due to the variety of topics in this publication, it is possible to encompass the widest possible area of interest and to contribute to the completion of a more complex state of research in the subject area. The authors of the publications are PhD students of the Department of Archaeology, the Department of Ethnology and Folklore, the Department of History and the Department of Culture and Tourism Management at the Faculty of Arts at the University of Constantine the Philosopher in Nitra.

Daniel Bešina

The evolution and formation of small settlements in Europe, with an emphasis on the territory of Slovakia

Abstract: The chapter presents the development of small medieval fortifications in a wide area of Europe. The development of medieval fortifications is briefly followed from the early Middle Ages to the Middle Ages. The problem is gradually narrowed down to the territory of Central Europe and finally, the development of medieval fortifications in the territory of Slovakia is more closely addressed.

Keywords: Middle Ages forts, terminology, motte, castles, nobility

The concept of medieval feudal settlements of a specific structural and functional form usually coincides with the concept of the castle, which is characteristic of the Gothic period. But upon closer observation it is clear that as a formation a medieval settlement is a significantly differentiated type of architecture. The structure of settlements depends on the time of creation, the type of feudalism and, of course, the function and importance of the settlement (Hejna 1965, 513). The most famous medieval fortifications were based on long-term socio-organizational and military needs. In general terms, they can be described as feudal settlements. From these facts, feudal settlements can be considered representative, administrative, organizational, military and economic units of monarchical institutions, and secular and ecclesiastical nobility.[1]

The form of the settlements was influenced by landscape. Situational placement depended on terrain morphology, usually based on the decision of the architect, who took into account contemporary customs and plans for settlement construction. The establishment of feudal settlements is associated with a phase in the social differentiation process in which a

---

1   Ruttkay, Čaplovič and Valašek, *Stredoveké feudálne sídla na Slovensku a ich hospodárske zázemi*, 241–254.

ruling class was created and its development was justified by the permanent land ownership of a growing number of wealthier vassals.

In terms of architecture, the development of manor houses usually derived from ancient traditions, prehistoric traditions applied in the domestic environment and, finally, simple experience that was a result of the effort to maximize the relief to protect the structure.[2]

It may be concluded that the basis of the mentioned building traditions was formed in the Frankish, Norman and Ottonian environment. At the end of this evolution and formation there were the medieval castles and rural settlements of the medieval nobility. The territory, when it came to the creation of feudal settlements, can be defined geographically from northern France across the Rhine into western and central Germany. Territory in southern Italy and Britain can be described as particular peripheral enclaves. In the earlier professional theses of researchers, antique influence was valued and emphasized. More recent results of archaeological research show a significant proportion of domestic traditions in the formation of medieval fortified settlements. Ancient tradition was rather limited to its own structural character of settlement. Domestic building traditions had already been developed in the initial formation of settlements, in terms of the definition of situation and form, and in the method of fortification and internal layout. The essence of local building traditions should be the subject of exploration throughout the European environment. Individual layers of the nobility had already appeared in the prehistoric period (Copper Age and later Bronze Age) and to them was closely connected differentiation from other emerging sectors of society. This led to the formation of divided settlement areas emphasizing higher social status.[3]

From an architectural point of view, the beginnings of European feudal settlements are usually searched for in Roman architecture, particularly in military and, partly, in civil architecture. The Roman military built structures at the borders of the empire. These smaller fenced points of the borders are in the expert sources described as "turris", "burgus" and "castellum". The terms refer to constructions of different form.

---

2 Hejna, *K situační a stavební formaci feudálního sídla v Evropě*, 513–583.
3 Hejna, *K situační a stavební formaci feudálního sídla v Evropě*, 583.

The term turris refers to a guard tower structure, which was a very important element in most of the border fortifications in Europe, Asia and North Africa.[4] Another structure of the Roman borders was the burgus. Unlike the guard tower turris, it represented a larger element in the defense system, but on the other hand, it is not possible to confuse it with the castellum.[5] In connection with the above-mentioned terms, the problems of the Roman military fortification of the castellum type can be briefly outlined. Originally, they were fortified with a mound and wooden construction or without fortification, and of various sizes ranging between 0.6 and 6 hectares. They were built according to the classical patterns of "castro" camps, but differed in the size of military unit located inside. Roman civil architecture played a role too – specifically the "villa rustica", a type of administrative rural settlement that was fortified with stone walls or by a mound.[6]

The impact of certain types of Roman military constructions on the formation of feudal settlements cannot be excluded. Importance and impact should be sought primarily in the sphere of architecture, particularly in terms of building technologies. Theories supporting the dominant influence of Antiquity have one serious weakness. Between the period of Roman building activities in Europe and the beginning of European feudal fortifications, we do not have enough knowledge about the direct impact or evolution of architecture.

This is the period between the 4th and 10th centuries AD, when there was serious political and social change (the disappearance of the western Roman Empire, and the great migration). In the archaeological research there is not enough information, especially about forms of settlements. Some continuity can be demonstrated in the sepultures, cult temples and fortifications of Roman military camps on the Rhine and Danube borders. Significant and fluent continuity can be seen in present-day France and Spain, arising from the old Roman "civitates", religious centers housing

---

4   Kiess, *Die Burgen in ihrer Funktion als Wohnbauten*, 28.
5   Kiess, *Die Burgen in ihrer Funktion als Wohnbauten*, 332; Radig, *Die Siedlungstypen in Deutschland*, 30.
6   Kiess, *Die Burgen in ihrer Funktion als Wohnbauten*, 332.

the seats of bishops. During the reign of the Merovingian dynasty, the first known royal settlements were formed on the ruins of camps.[7]

Previously, it was mentioned that more intensive research on fortified settlements and deeper interest in the issue place an increasing emphasis on prehistoric building traditions in the formation of feudal settlements. These beginnings we can find already in the late Stone Age. From the end of the ancient period, one cannot fail to mention the influence of Celtic structural elements acting on both sides of the Roman border. It may be concluded that there was influence and exchange of building traditions between Celtic and Roman culture. Celtic society was considerably differentiated – it had its own ruling class with their own settlements. In connection with the Celtic environment, Romanization also appeared in the fortified courts of the Celtic nobility. In this context, it is important to mention the rural abodes of the Irish environment, called "crannogs", situated on an artificial dam in marshy areas. From the same provenance came "raths", which represented settlements on upland sites fortified with a mound and ditch. From the southern German region, we have the "Viereckschanzen" fortified residence of tetrahedral shape, probably of Celtic origin. Due to their small amount of settlement diversity, they have rather an iconic significance.[8] Germanic architecture would become part of certain types of feudal court in the form of Germanic hall construction. This was a longitudinal one-room space, and it is noteworthy that this appeared in the British Isles along with the Anglo-Saxon invasion.

This type of construction became part of the fenced courts in the pre-Romanesque period. From the coastal areas of northern Europe also comes the structure called a "wurta" (or warten, terpen). They were mostly situated on flat terrain. The origin of wurta is from prehistoric times, where it was possible to see the building of artificial dams and this phenomenon lasted until recently. Wurta settlements had a rural character; therefore they cannot be cited as an example of feudal forms of fortification. Situational forms, such as an artificially screeded hill, which could be

---

7   Hejna, *K situační a stavební formaci feudálního sídla v Evropě*, 513–583.
8   Filip, *Keltové ve střední Evropě*, 551.

affected by certain buildings of the lords' settlements mostly in the Anglo-Saxon and Frankish context, cannot be overlooked.[9]

An individual group with considerable influence was the Saxon castles. In the area of Saxony, along with the large castles, there were smaller structures, frequently built with brick and with a circular layout with buildings around the perimeter. The central courtyard of the internal area was open and different from the karolinska castles in terms of the flatness of the area.[10] Saxon castles provide a more complete and important type of settlement. They were built on inaccessible terrain and builders emphasized the strong outer walls. The fortifications were built on an embankment with a wooden construction. The origins of the Saxon castles date back to the period of war between Saxons and Charlemagne and their appearance corresponded with prehistoric building traditions.

Saxon castles are an important and characteristic group of buildings, the existence of which lasted until the 11th century. This group of fortified settlements were, mainly in the older literature, considered as essential in the placement and construction of settlements in the territory inhabited by Slavs, bordering the Carolingian and later Ottonian Empire.[11] German researchers (Müller-Wille, 1966) concluded, based on years of research that among the Saxon castles there were two basic groups in the area of Saxony and Thuringia, as well as central Europe.

The persistence of the ancient culture can be observed mainly in the Franconian region, in particular in the formation of Merovingian culture. As an example it is possible to take the settlement of Merovingian kings verified by archaeological research in Quierey in Soissone, where continuity of settlement had occurred from the Roman period till the arrival of the Franks. This event is followed by the evolution of settlement units, which can be called courts. The court in the Merovingian and Frankish period grew on the basis of antique rural villas and building traditions in

9   Reinerth, *Vorgeschichte der deutschen Stämme*, 367 s.; Kiess, *Die Burgen in ihrer Funktion als Wohnbauten,* 35.

10 Hejna, *České tvrze,* 15.

11 Radig, *Die Siedlungstypen in Deutschland,*183; Rahtz, *The Saxon and Medieval Palaces at Cheddar,* 53; Hejna, *K situační a stavební formaci feudálního sídla v Evropě,* 524.

upland fortified settlements. Frankish written sources put the creation of
the first settlements in the 7th century, when the royal entourage evolved
into a certain social class, endowed with ranks and landed property, which
was previously part of the royal estate.[12]

In western Europe, there exists in written sources from the Early Middle
Ages (from the time of the Merovingians), specific mention of the existence
and construction of fortified settlements, which later evolved into medieval feudal settlements. In the old provincial areas appears the Frankish
court building "curtis regalis". A Frankish court was characteristic, in
contrast to the Roman model, of the construction of a certain peristyle
type in each separate part, located inside a square fenced area. This phenomenon is identified with domestic building traditions or with influence
taken from the shape of the Roman camps. Typical elements of the structure – the house, farm buildings and fortifications – are not only the oldest
type of settlement of its kind in western Europe, but also form the basis for
further development of medieval feudal residences, built with a clear application of ancient building traditions.[13] A significant factor in the spread
of Frankish court buildings was mainly the expansion of power of the
Frankish Empire under Charlemagne in the years 772–804. The difficult
problem of the infiltration of Frankish building tradition into the construction of courts and castles in conquered areas led to a detailed analysis
of written sources, and the results of the research including topographic
data and various archaeological findings. The Carolingian period should
in addition to courts and castles be remembered for a building that is in
its architectural form was original. The Carolingian palace has its origin
in the Merovingian period and it is a testament to the progressive differentiation of fortified settlements. The palace had an earlier settlement and
courtly character, in contrast with courts, which had mostly a watchtower
function. The palace represented the power of the sovereign and therefore
satisfied the requirements of court life. The original Carolingian palace is
known in French, German, Bavarian and Northern Italian contexts.[14]

---

12 Kiess, *Die Burgen in ihrer Funktion als Wohnbauten*, 332; Uslar, *Studien zu
     frühgeschichtlichen Befestigungen zwischen Nordsee und Alpen*, 290.
13 Jankuhn, *Die frühmittelalterliche Seehandelspätze im Nord-und Ostseeraum*, 6.
14 Kiess, *Die Burgen in ihrer Funktion als Wohnbauten*, 45.

In central and eastern Europe, fortified settlements evolved independently, even without the direct influence of the Roman building tradition. At the turn of 5th–6th century, Slavic tribes settled in the territories. After the 8th century, when Slavic society had reached a certain degree of social evolution, forts had become not only common, but merely a typical abode. Within the fortification there was allocated the dwelling of an earl and this lasted for some time until neighboring noble residences were built which separated the settlements of lesser nobles as a reflection of the emerging feudal fragmentation.[15]

Fortified settlements of the Slavs in eastern Europe can be encountered from the 8th century. On the territory of present-day Ukraine, Russia and Belarus was the oldest Slavic fortified settlement from the 8th to 10th century located mostly on promontory projections or on river islands. In that earlier period, the Slavic fort had not already been recorded as a separately divided court, or other specific structure on the premises or outside.[16] More complex division of position, form and size was developed in fortified areas in the period from the 10th to 13th century. The older forts of the Kievan Rus were assimilated into the old Russian "Gorod", which represented crafts, commercial and peasant settlements. A large group of fortified settlements were represented by buildings whose size and shape was dictated by an artificial mound and ditch without being directly subordinate to the natural topography. For that type of construction, most characteristic was a circular, tetrahedral or sometimes semi-circular shape with a small footprint and enclosed fenced area.[17] In the 10th–13th century, we observe in the whole East Slav area strong growth of medium-sized localities situated mostly on elevated promontory positions, as well as lowland marshy terrain. All these facts lead to the conclusion that the development of small princely courts in the Rus resulted from deep social changes related to the strengthening of the feudal social changes among the eastern Slavs.[18] According to the findings of P. Tretyakov, N.[19], it is

---

15 Hensel, *Archeologia o początkach miast słowiańskich*, 187.
16 Grekov, *Kyjevská Rus*; Tretjakov, *U kolébky staré rusy*, 347.
17 Hejna, *K situační a stavební formaci feudálního sídla v Evropě*, 535.
18 Hejna, *K situační a stavební formaci feudálního sídla v Evropě*, 535.
19 Tretjakov, *U kolébky staré rusy*, 347.

possible to record aristocratic courts' elevated position from the 8th century. In a similar vein, the idea that fortified villages and castles formed from the 8th century onwards from armed retinues to the courts of a feudal magnate was posited by another researcher, B. D. Grekov.[20]

Research on the territory of Kievan Rus fully correlates with the data found by Polish archaeologists. The development of feudalism in Poland was a decisive period in the second half of the 10th century, when there was a conversion of old settlements of tribal princes to new aristocratic castles, built on a territorial basis.[21] From the 11th century, the older administrative center began to accrue castles (civitates, castella) with a guarding function, rarely built with an increased inner area. Castles as real feudal settlements were built from the 12th century, and especially from the 13th century they were created in the periphery of older centers – namely newly settled areas.[22]

No later than from the second half of the 10th century, a turning point in the evolution of fortified settlements occurred between the Oder and Elbe, as in Poland. From existing tribal centers there were created, in addition to large fortified settlements, relatively small fortified settlements of Slavic nobles. These small circular castles, mostly of a ring type, were built in the lowland and upland environment. From the end of the 12th century, the settlements of German feudal lords were built on their foundations. A similar situation also occurred in the territory of Lausitz and Saxony.[23]

In the Slavic region, there are circular fortified formations of old origin, as evidenced by study of Polish and Sliezka castles originating in the 7th and 8th centuries. An example of an ancient circuit castle with a fortified circular area with a residential unit inside the area is Tornow in eastern Germany. Therefore, it can be assumed that if a circular fortification in the 8th century in the Slavic environment were substantiated, it was probably also undertaken by the Saxons.

---

20 Grekov, *Kyjevská Rus*, 580.
21 Hejna, *K situační a stavební formaci feudálního sídla v Evropě*, 539.
22 Kamińska, *Grodziska stożkowate sladem posiadłości rycerskich XIII - XIV wieku*, 44–45.
23 Hejna, *K situační a stavební formaci feudálního sídla v Evropě*, 550.

During the 9th century, a certain type of fortification represented by an artificial circular embankment called a "motte" achieved the next stage of development. Fortified formations of the motte type consisted of an artificial embankment, replacing a natural ridge, which would protect residential buildings on top of a hill. Mottes were largely concentrated in the flatlands of Great Britain to the eastern regions of Germany. They are considered to be forerunners of medieval water castles.[24] Lowland motte-type castles were mostly part of a larger fortified area. The artificially formed body of the motte, usually featuring a wooden tower, had a centrally or eccentrically located position toward the fortified forecastle with a different layout. They could be rounded, square, oval, rectangle or of irregular shape depending on the environment and the manner of construction. The bailey was created by structures of a farming nature (stables and craftsmen's workshops).[25]

The most significant part of the motte complex consisted of a residential tower building on an artificial hill, and thus together they created a new situational element that influenced the form of feudal seats throughout the European region. At first the origin of the motte was identified mainly with the antique building tradition especially with towers on the Roman border. More recent data makes it clear that the origins can be found after the end of the 9th century, in the 10th century in areas west and south of the Rhine.[26] The building of artificial embankments was preferred mostly on flat terrain in the lowlands or in the immediate vicinity of the watercourse, which only increased the potential of the building's defenses. In connection with the construction of the tower on top of the embankment is derived the word "motte", of unclear etymological origin. It tallies with the Normans, who started to build their settlements in northern Europe from the second decade of the 10th century, after the conclusion of the peace of St. Clair in 911. The view of H. Hinz, who considers the "rundwall" and "motte" types of settlement as a display of the same tendency of water vicinity use to protect the settlement, appears most believable.[27] This led to the

---

24 Novotný et al., *Encyklopédia archeology,* 579.
25 Jaššo, *Stredoveké hrádky na západnom Slovensku,* 129.
26 Hinz, *Motte und Donjon,* 131; Hejna, *K situační a stavební formaci feudálního sídla v Evropě,* 557.
27 Hinz, *Motte und Donjon,* 131.

improvement of the circular castle by the motte, as can be seen in the small castle of Husterknupp. Compared to the simple circular castle, the motte is a specialized situational form of settlement. Its discovery in the system of fortified settlements meant a certain type of situational disposition.[28] The origin of the motte cannot be clearly deduced from only one particular context. Initial classification into the system of feudal settlements took place in the territory west and south of the Rhine of the ancient traditions, in the Frankish and Norman environment. In the English terminology, fortified artificially built circular mounds are known as a "keep-and-bailey castles". It is a fortified formation based on a subsoil motte. Some fortified circular formations were likely to have been built before the Norman invasion, originating in the domestic Irish-Scottish traditions: as an example, after the year 1050 the Hereford and similar Totnes castles, which in contrast to the typical motte were a combination of a circular castle with a motte. The difference was in the upper part, where there was no tower construction in the circular palisade, but the palisade itself had become part of the settlement layout, similar to Saxon castles. Wooden structures formed around the outer rampart a ring which formed inside a small open area. This scheme is in Anglo-Saxon termed a "shell-keep" and it grew up next to the classic Franco-Norman donjon. A prime example of a "shell-keep" is the Restormel stone castle with a diameter of 40 meters and a circumferential ring with a width of 7 meters. A castle with a tower on raised terrain is named "Turmhügel" (Burghügel), but it should be noted that this term cannot be regarded as uniform because of imprecise definitions. In southern Germany, they are usually described by the term "Buhl".[29] The term "Hausberg" refers to all the castles on raised terrain in Lower Austria.[30] In Poland, they are named "grody stożkowa".[31]

In the German terminology, the terms are considered synonyms but P. Grimm distinguishes the names "Turmhügel" and "Burghügel". A free-standing tower settlement "Turmhügel" is subordinated to the term

---

28 Hejna, *K situační a stavební formaci feudálního sídla v Evropě*, 558.

29 Hejna, *K situační a stavební formaci feudálního sídla v Evropě*, 575.

30 Schadn, *Die Hausberge und verwandten Wehranlagen in Niederösterreich*, 20–24.

31 Kamińska, *Grodziska stożkowate sladem posiadłości rycerskich XIII - XIV wieku*, 43–46.

"Burghüge" which includes all fortified settlements in a raised position. Most researchers derive the "Turmhügel" from "motta", from the Franco-Norman region in northern France. In large and medium-sized examples we can observe a built-up area around the perimeter-tracking palisade or wall. The tower on the embankment in the middle of the site is mainly a smaller formation. These differences in construction are a basic criterion for internal segmentation. The common element is a raised embankment with a settlement that was sequentially applied on natural slopes and hills.[32] From the central German region, the tower castle arrived along the Danube to the area of Austria quite early.

The region of Lower Austria was, in the Early Middle Ages, part of the Slavic settlement area on the central Danube, undoubtedly belonging to the advanced central area of Great Moravia. Two structures were found here. At the beginning of the 20th century their original purpose was very unclear. The dominant opinion was that they were cult structures of the Quads and Rugias and after gradual research they were recognized as feudal castles.[33] The situation in Lower Austria was described in detail by H. P. Schaden.[34] In his own words he very extensively reviewed the remains of small feudal castles. An example is Drösing from the mid-11th century – a bipartite castle with a rounded motte with a diameter of 35 meters, and the still undated Oberrhausen, also a type of bipartite castle with a diameter motte of 40 meters.[35]

Written sources from the 11th to 12th centuries tell us quite clearly about the design and interiors of the tower castles. In addition to written sources, we have even rare pictorial sources, of which the most famous is the tapestry of Bayeux, where even the building of a small castle is captured. On a rare woven painting, there have been identified a Dinant castle made from wood, with vertical beams with a tower on a raised embankment and surrounding buildings attached to the tower. From written sources there is only the record of Tartarius, who writes about castle Chatillou sur Loire, belonging to Sequin. The building is described as a "towering structure

32 Hejna, *K situační a stavební formaci feudálního sídla v Evropě*, 576.
33 Nekuda and Unger, *Hrádky a tvrze na Moravě*, 20.
34 Schadn, *Die Hausberge und verwandten Wehranlagen in Niederösterreich*, 268.
35 Schadn, *Die Hausberge und verwandten Wehranlagen in Niederösterreich*, 268.

made from wood, because the Lord of this small castle was strong and
came from a wealthy local family" The tower had an upstairs room – a
solarium occupied by the owner and his family. Downstairs was a room
with many storage vessels. The solarium had a wooden floor.[36] From the
early 12th century there is the preserved record of John of Colmieu, which
states that "next to the hall of the church was a kind of castle very high
and built according to the habit of the land (Belgium) many years ago".
Further he writes: "It is customary for the wealthy and prominent people
in this country, the more you have the habit of living in enmity and war,
the more likely they are building a fortified residence for their own safety,
to maintain their own authority, to suppress the peers or for the oppression of their vassals..."

In the Danube region, as in central Germany, the motte would eventually come into contact with Slavic settlement. In the 11th century, only
very rare evidence of motte occurrence can be cited, but until now evidence
dating back to more widespread occurrence of mottes in central Europe
dates from the 12th to the 13th century. The motte influenced the adjust-
ment of old circular residential buildings of simple or complex character.
Secondarily they occurred in the corners of older fortified settlements with
residential, guarding and defensive functions, or a central function in the
area of smaller circular castles with a large fortress.[37] A well-known and
typical motte from the Lower Rhine is Husterknupp. In Hoverberg an
interesting castle has been reviewed.[38] Important archaeological research in
Gommerstedte has shown the close relationship of lower nobility to individual farming. The existence of a castle on Gommerstedte in Böslebene
dates back to the 11th–12th century.[39]

Progress in Lower Austria is wholly consistent with the spread of
building traditions in Moravia where the oldest building of this kind
already dates back to the 12th and the first half of the 13th century.[40]

---

36 Hejna, *České tvrze*, 11.
37 Hejna, *K situační a stavební formaci feudálního sídla v Evropě*, 577.
38 Nekuda and Unger, *Hrádky a tvrze na Moravě*, 366; Herrnbrodt, *Stand der frühmittelalterlichen Mottenforschung im Rheinland*, 77–100.
39 Timpel, *Gommerstedt bei Bösleben, Kr. Arnstadt. Burghügel und Siedlung des Mittelalter*, 142–144; Nekuda and Unger, *Hrádky a tvrze na Moravě*, 13.
40 Schadn, *Die Hausberge und verwandten Wehranlagen in Nie derösterreich*, 268.

Their spread and development reached the Austrian Danube region from the southern German region where the motte had existed since the 11th century.[41] One of the reasons for the proliferation of this type of residence through each area was a certain advance in the process of feudalization.[42]

In the Czech region, a relatively large number of courts (fortresses) were maintained, which with their size, double ditches and mounds revealed a considerable range of earthworks. Historical and archaeological research informs us of their form. Among the many works about Czech courts, the work by A. Hejna *České tvrze* excels.[43] The author briefly describes 250 localities of which 61 are photographically documented. The situation in the Czech region before the 13th century suggests that the courts and castles cannot be solely considered settlements of minor feudal lords.

The data in written sources rather refers to ownership by a monarch or wealthy ecclesiastical or secular feudal lord. Changes come in the 13th century, when the number of small nobility settlements of a certain type increased. Frequently, the only building in the complex was a fortified tower built of wood or stone.[44] The oldest form of small fortified settlements in the Czech Republic can be observed in the private courts in the fort at Štítor and probably in the left fort in Stará Boleslav and Prague Castle (the Bishop's court and the court of the priest Pavol). Some courts from the 13th century had buildings built to the peripheral wall of the fortress. This type of court we find in Martinice near Votice.[45] At the same time there was an interesting type of court in the territory of the Czech region, in whose fortifications a church was built. In a part of this area, there were farm buildings also. The mentioned type of court was archaeologically documented in Chvojň in Benešov.[46] The gradual disappearance

41 Müller-Wille, *Mittelalterliche Burghugel im nordlichen Rheinland*, 113; Hinz, *Motte und Donjon*, 131.
42 Kouřil, Měřinský and Plaček, *Opevněná sídla na Moravě a ve Slezku(vznik, vývoj, význam, funkce, současný stav a perspektivy dalšího výzkumu)*, 129.
43 Hejna, *České tvrze*, 179.
44 Nekuda and Unger, *Hrádky a tvrze na Moravě*, 366; Herrnbrodt, *Stand der frühmittelalterlichen Mottenforschung im Rheinland*, 16.
45 Nekuda and Unger, *Hrádky a tvrze na Moravě*, 18.
46 Kašička, *Tvrze středních Čech: Středisko Státní památkové péče a ochrany přírody středočeského kraje*, 60.

of court settlements with tribunes' churches happened in the 13th century as one of the consequences of major economic and social change. Another type of court was the discovery uncovered by research in Zvírotice, where the court was protected by a moat and it was possible to enter the tower via a gateway. Two towers stood in two corners of the fortification and in the other corner was located a residential building. Similar courts were built in the 15th century, but more attention was devoted to the fortifications as a result of the extension of conflict.[47]

From the late Middle Ages there appear in some settlements rich architectural elements linked to courts, and their traditional economic facilities oriented toward associated industries, for example beer brewing, sheep farming, viticulture, fruit growing, etc.[48] Medieval manor courts played an important role in the economy of the medieval village. They are a special feature in the structure of villages from a manufacturing, spatial and construction standpoint. The historical background and common destinies of the Czech Republic, Moravia and Silesia should encourage deeper attention and study of material sources.[49]

The evolution of the medieval feudal settlement in central and western Europe has not been entirely fluent and has been influenced by many factors. An important change was the tendency toward an upland location and for the construction of stronger fortifications, where we can include the construction of stone fortifications and of settlements from stone towers or of a morphologically different character. Castles gradually became solely settlements of feudal lords and their families.[50]

Great Moravian manorial courts

Approximately from the middle of the 8th century, there was a merging of territorially smaller principalities into larger units, and this process accompanied the formation of nobles' and princes' fortified settlements.[51] The

47 Nekuda and Unger, *Hrádky a tvrze na Moravě*, 19.
48 Kašička, *Tvrze středních Čech: Středisko Státní památkové péče a ochrany přírody středočeského kraje*, 61.
49 Chotěbor and Smetánka, *Panské dvory na české vesnici*, 47.
50 Hejna, *České tvrze*, 17.
51 Ruttkay, *Sídla spoločenských elít na strednom Ponitrí v 9. - 13. Storočí*, 77.

Moravian organizational structure from the 9th century cannot be judged by one model or generalization. Specific local and territorial features of evolution played an important role in the differentiation of the entire organizational structure. Nitra can be marked as a "castle city" (civitas) in light of the current research. Besides the prince and court nobility, members of military retinues belonged to the leading groups in Great Moravian society.

The retinue probably consisted of members of the nobility or members of newer military forces with layers of freemen. The power of manors grew during the reign of Svätopluk I. The military retinue as a newly emerging element formed, in terms of military service, part of the prince's army. Power and separatist conflicts between members of the new nobility could manifest themselves at critical times, as after the death of Svätopluk I, when there was an internal conflict which resulted in the ruin of the fragile structure of the country.[52] From archaeologically explored courts, it is obvious that full organizational value was achieved by courts after the middle of the 9th century.[53] In terms of evidence in particular palisade fortifications, the geometric footprint of the area, the presence of secular and religious buildings and the overall diversity of buildings from the surrounding peasant or production houses can be observed. A particular problem in the case of land survey is to identify palisades. For this reason, courts were recognized in central Europe much later than forts. Locating palisade trenches is only possible with systematic archaeological research and with soil under suitable scientific conditions, as was the case for example in Břeclav-Pohansko.

Central European courts from the 9th century have their closest analogy particularly in the Franconian area, but we cannot speak about a direct continuity. They primarily reflect the social elements in the evolution of central European medieval aristocracy. The social superiority of courts owners should be demonstrated by their location.[54] Small forts (castles) probably functioned as smaller local centers or had a guarding function. Some smaller and partly different fortified hill-forts (castles) could fulfill

---

52 Ruttkay, *Sídla spoločenských elít na strednom Ponitrí v 9. - 13. Storočí*, 79.
53 Ruttkay, *Sídla spoločenských elít na strednom Ponitrí v 9. - 13. Storočí*, 78.
54 Ruttkay, *Sídla spoločenských elít na strednom Ponitrí v 9. - 13. Storočí.*, 80.

the function of courts, which could be described as some form of early
medieval castle.[55] A direct clue to the existence of courts exists in several
Great Moravian locations. Near the princely court in Mikulčice and in
Staré Město were smaller settlements of nobles. So far, we know three
cases in which courts constituted a separate functional unit, and that they
were solitary buildings.[56]

In Moravia is perhaps the best studied Great Moravian court, in Břeclav-
Pohansko.[57] The court in Pohansko probably represented the fledgling center
of an early feudal manor, where dues were collected. The identified housing
stock allows one to suspect that the inhabitant of the court did not directly
deal with agriculture but that they primarily organized agricultural production as landowners. Buildings were relatively large, mostly of an above-
ground character, or with an intricate post-hole construction arranged in
regular rows, or functional units.[58] These purpose-built groups of buildings
were used as a specialist craft zone or as a space for autonomous economic
entities.[59]

In Slovakia, two Great Moravian courts have been studied, in Ducové
and Nitrianska Blatnica.[60] The courts in Ducové and Nitrianska Blatnica
represented new formations which arose probably around the middle of
the 9th century and took over the guarding function from older extinct
castles. Both courts arose after the fall of Great Moravia, but neither of
them had the characteristics of direct continuity to the Middle Ages.[61] The
location of churches in the areas of settlements and the related ownership
of churches such as the rotunda in Ducové and Nitrianska Blatnica bear
witness to the adopting of a new religion "from above".[62]

---

55 Šalkovský, *K problematike opevnených sídiel vo včasnom stredoveku na
    Slovensku*, 60.
56 Ruttkay, *Slovensko vo včasnom stredoveku*, 137.
57 Dostál, *Břeclav - Pohansko. Velkomoravský veľmožský dvorec IV*, 243–247.
58 Dostál, *Břeclav - Pohansko. Velkomoravský veľmožský dvorec IV*, 247.
59 Dresler and Přichystalová, *Břeclav - Pohansko. Veľkomoravské hradisko
    2014*, 47.
60 Ruttkay, *Výskum včasnostredovekého opevneného sídla v Ducovom, okres
    Trnava*, 138.
61 Ruttkay, Ruttkay and Šalkovský, *Slovensko vo včasnom stredoveku*, 138–139.
62 Ruttkay, *Sídla spoločenských elít na strednom Ponitrí v 9. - 13. Storočí*, 82;
    Ruttkay, *Včasnostredoveký sídliskový komplex a Rotunda sv. Juraja pri*

In connection with the previously mentioned knowledge of the Great Moravian courts, one cannot fail to mention the discovery of the courts in Transdanubia in the center of the Pannonian manor of Zalavár. The mentioned court was found in the location of Borjúallás, originally situated on a slightly emerged island, which stood out from the swampy terrain on the southern edge of Lake Balaton (Blaten).[63] Finds from graves, mostly personal items, suggest a possible link with the territory of Moravia, while weapons and riding gear are characteristic of Carolingian art.[64] The author of the study, R. Müller,[65] described the court as "Carolingian".

Due to previously known information from the review of the Great Moravian courts (Ducové, Nitrianska Blatnica and by uncertain indications Dražovce), it can be stated that fortified villages with various forms of buildings were a common type of private residence and represented a higher social class in the early Hungarian period. Uphill variants of courts often merge functionally and also terminologically into the category of castles.[66]

From the research of northern castle areas in Slovakia emerge surprising results. An upland area of a court type with a masonry structure has managed to be partially uncovered at Trenčín castle, whose origins are from the mid-11th century.[67] At Spiš Castle there has also been discovered much older monumental architecture dating back further than the castle itself, a Romanesque castle from the first half of the 13th century. The origins of the mentioned locations (similar to the situation of potential continuity sketches in Bojnice and Brekove) date back before the period of the gradual connecting of Slovakia to the Hungarian state. The situation may

Nitrianskej Blatnici, 55–61; Dorica, *Rotunda sv. Juraja pri Nitrianskej Blatnici. Jej nové miesto medzi najstaršími sakrálnymi stavbami na Slovensku*, 62–67; Ruttkay, *Správa o výskume v Nitrianskej Blatnici v roku 1980: výskumná správa*, 256–258.

63 Szőke, *Pannónia a Karoling-korban. In: Akadémiai doktori értekezés tézisei*, 6.
64 Štefanovičová, *Blatnohrad. Osudy Pribinu a Koceľa po opustení Nitrianska*, 76.
65 R. Müller, *Karoling udvarház és temetője*, 91–98.
66 Ruttkay, Čaplovič and Vallašek, *Stredoveké feudálne sídla na Slovensku a ich hospodárske zázemie*, 246.
67 Nešporová, *Výsledky historicko-archeologického výskumu na Trenčianskom hrade*, 142–143.

be similar also at other locations, but we cannot yet talk about the direct continuity of the organizational structure of the Great Moravian period.[68]

Political and cultural development after the collapse of the Great Moravian Empire in the territory of Slovakia took place in two different areas. Southern territories in the early 10th century came under the control of old Hungarian veterans. Some of the former large military centers (Nitra, Bratislava, Starý Tekov) remained with the same level of fortification and during the 10th–11th centuries they were rebuilt into district (comitates) castles.[69] Northerly locations remained largely in the periphery of the old Hungarian ethnic group and were incorporated into the emerging early Hungarian feudal state only during the 11th and 12th centuries.[70]

Evolution of small manor houses in Slovakia in the High and Late Middle Ages

The settlements of the minor rural nobility were the clearest expression of the advancing wealth and social differentiation of the medieval countryside.

The minor nobility had been forming since the 11th century from castle warriors, vassals and villeins and the impoverished nobility.[71]

The territory of Slovakia had started to integrate into the emerging Hungarian state after the year 1018, i.e., from the second half of the reign of King Stephan I. Signs of hereditary land ownership along with servants and own military entourage held by nobles (maiores) date back to the first half of the 11th century. Courts are first mentioned in written sources from the 10th century, where they have a double meaning.

They exist as either a royal court or a settlement with established populations forming an economic center with significant property and with a particular organizational structure. In the properties held by secular feudal lords the courts (curia, curtis) appeared in the 11th and intensified

---

68 Ruttkay, Čaplovič and Vallašek, *Stredoveké feudálne sídla na Slovensku a ich hospodárske zázemie*, 246.
69 Ruttkay, *Sídla spoločenských elít na strednom Ponitrí v 9. - 13. Storočí*, 82.
70 Kučera, *Sociálna štruktúra obyvateľstva Slovenska v 10.-12. Storočí*, 53.
71 Habovštiak, *Stredoveká dedina na Slovensku*, 122; Kučera, *Sociálna štruktúra obyvateľstva Slovenska v 10.-12. Storočí*, 28.

only in the 12th century.[72] Courts in the Middle Ages represented a complex of buildings with economic and administrative or guarding function. Constructions comprised of the lord's abode, along with servant dwellings, or those for retinue or slaves. The private residence of the lord at a later period became separated from the farmyard and there emerged fortified castles and castles with a significant military function.[73] In written sources from the 11th century they mention manor houses, more precisely courts, as the oldest form of settlement of high nobility. The difference between courts and castles is mainly that in courts we can find the remains of natural fortifications.[74] M. Kučera considers it certain that court organization was built on the economically more advanced territory occupied by the Slavic ethnic group; this suggests a longer-term development of the court's genesis.[75] Development of the court organization was mainly in the 12th century, and written sources from the early 13th century attest to its gradual disintegration, but this issue is answered only marginally. The first mention of a specific court is from the year 1061 in the Somogy district, alongside comprehensive private property. The oldest record from Slovakia about the interiors and villages themselves comes from the testament of the old Hunt-Poznan branch of the monastery in Hronský Beňadik, dating to 1165. In Slepčany, there is a mention of an orchard and a mill belonging to the manor house. From the 11th and 12th centuries through royal grants, these cities become the property of the church and secular lords. Examples include the old royal court in Pastovce, from the second half of the 11th century belonging to the wealthy Hunt-Poznan clan. In the leading strata of society in the first half of the 11th century it is possible to recognize the lower nobility, who owned smaller properties. They were in a militarily dependent employment relationship with the king. As well as the monarch, the lower nobility were linked to a higher secular or ecclesiastical feudal lord via a vassal relationship. Evidence of the relatively large lower layer of feudal lords from the 11th century is

---

72 Kučera, *Slovensko po páde Veľkej Morave,* 367.
73 Novotný et al., *Encyklopédia archeology,* 211–212.
74 Fiala, Habovštiak and Štefanovičová, *Opevnené sídliská z 10. - 13. storočia na Slovensku,* 437.
75 Kučera, *Slovensko po páde Veľkej Moravy,* 368.

provided by the testament of Lambert of the Hunt-Poznan family from
1132 to the Bezovicka monastery, which lists a number of properties purchased by Lambert from minor feudal lords. Interesting records in connection with inherited property are mentioned in connection with the death
of Stoislav. The nobleman died in 1185 on a Bela III expedition in the
Balkans. Stoislav had no heirs and therefore King Bela III gave lifetime use
of his estate to his mother, which was quite a remarkable act, because in
other cases the property would usually be acquired by the crown.

The estate in Upper Nitra (included in the estate was also Nitrianska
Blatnica) was gained by the Bishopric of Nitra after the death of Stoislav's
mother.[76] From the 11th and 12th century, villages become the property of
the church and secular nobility.[77]

To the royal courts became appended royal servant settlements, which
represented a typical component of their territorial spread throughout the
country.[78] The property of the king was managed by the monarch, and a
system of courts and servant settlements consolidated his organizational
apparatus. This controlling and adapting of the organization demonstrates
the strict functioning of the country, not least the low social division
of labor.

The sovereign was thus forced to wander with his army and court
across the kingdom, while the services of the inhabitants of royal servant
settlements and courts were used.[79]

In the first Code of Štefan I, the "curia regalis" – the royal court – is mentioned. The record comes from the years before 1038 and an early stage
is possible to find at the turn of the 10th and 11th centuries. Royal courts
featured from the end of the 10th century as one of the determinants of
royal power. Functionally a royal court is a power center, but also the economic center of the surrounding villages with their subjects. For optimal
function of the royal servant organization, the court economic hub was
a base. In case of the stay of the ruler in the area, courts were also residential private settlements.[80] The small number of written sources greatly

76 Ruttkay, *Sídla spoločenských elít na strednom Ponitrí v 9. - 13. Storočí,* 83.
77 Ruttkay, Ruttkay and Šalkovský, *Slovensko vo včasnom stredoveku,* 144.
78 Kučera, *Slovensko po páde Veľkej Moravy,* 373.
79 Kučera, *Slovensko po páde Veľkej Moravy,* 381.
80 Ruttkay, Ruttkay and Šalkovský, *Slovensko vo včasnom stredoveku,*144.

limits the obtaining of a more accurate picture about the deployment of courts, in particular in properties which did not change owner. There is a crucial role for research in the future, especially archaeology, which can give us specific information about the organization of courts in Early Medieval Hungary.[81]

During archaeological excavations, these settlements are usually found in urban or rural medieval villages. There are occasions when they occur also at greater distances from villages. Buildings inside rural settlements are detected without significant trace of natural fortification. Notable is their difference from villein abodes in the village. They differ in their larger dimensions, siting on uphill ground, complicated construction and also material basis.[82] In terms of archaeological research, there has not been much success in finding one of these settlements from the early Hungarian period, although several royal courts were identified in the field (for example, in the vanished colony of Dvorčany, Šoporňa, Tešedíkova, the Court of Zittau). In connection with the royal court, it is necessary to mention the upland settlements of a court type with a significant fortification pattern performing a watchtower function. A border-guarding function on the Hungarian-Czech border was also performed by the lowland Wyvar on the Morava River in Holíč.[83] So far the only indication of the Hungarian aspect of the royal court was in Zirec near Veszprém. In this court died King Andrew II in 1061. In 1182, King Bela II gave the court with its church to the Cistercian Order. The court was built over several phases. There were recognized remnants of a large secular building with a larger church and even remnants of a stone perimeter wall. The diameter of the circular court area was 80 meters. Koppány declares that the court in Zirec was already of pre-Hungarian origin, as evidenced by the finding of residues of wooden beams of the church, which was replaced in the 11th century by a new stone church.[84]

In Slovakia, there are preconditions for the existence of courts in Dvory nad Žitavou, mentioned in 1075 as the property of a new monastery in

81 Kučera, *Slovensko po páde Veľkej Moravy*, 368.
82 Habovštiak, *Stredoveká dedina na Slovensku*, 122–123.
83 Čaplovič, *Stredoveké feudálne sídla na Slovensku a ich hospodárske zázemie*, 83.
84 Koppány, *XI. századi királyi udvarház maradványai Zircen*, 142.

Hronský Beňadik. In the location of Palota in Hrhov, archaeologists managed to discover a court acting as a royal residence in the second half of the 13th century. In the location of Palota near Šoporňa was, based on field observation, a localized court with vestiges of defunct architecture. Not all royal courts referred to in the documents have been possible to locate. Such a case is the court in Pastovce, which the king had already in the last quarter of the 11th century given to a person of high nobility, and later, in 1132, through the Lambert donations it was given to the monastery in Bzovík. Before the 13th century there are mentioned other hitherto undiscovered royal courts, for example, in Nitra – Dolné Krškany (Dvorčany-Curtoiz), Tešedíkovo (Udvardi rét) and Boleráz near Krušovice (Zequi). Some toponyms also inform us about a possible court (dvorníky, udvarház, yard, porch, palace...).[85]

From the 11th century, as well as the district centers, also other fortified focal points served to protect the territory of the kingdom or to protect important roads, fords, mountain passes and also new colonized territory. These small fortification structures were situated in strategic positions. Construction was initially formed by timber towers with supports, protected by a moat or also with a wooden or stone mound. Such structures were the castle in Nitra-Chrenová (Mačací zámok), in Kamenín (Várhegy) and in Malé Kosihy.[86] The tower initially consisted of multiple functions (residential and economic). Based on the results of locality research there can be seen a gradual transfer of functions to the newly constructed buildings arising out of the tower. This leads to a widening of the area of the whole construction. Smaller medieval strongholds and courts were gradually rebuilt and adapted to the new conditions of warfare and housing (Topoľčianky, Partizánske-Šimonovany).[87]

Till the 12th century, they were classified on the basis of the remarkable results of archaeological research on the nobles of Velčice and also the lowland court in Bratislava-Dúbravka, with origins from the beginning the

---

85 Ruttkay, Ruttkay and Šalkovský, *Slovensko vo včasnom stredoveku,* 145.
86 Ruttkay, Čaplovič and Vallašek, *Stredoveké feudálne sídla na Slovensku a ich hospodárske zázemie,* 247.
87 Ruttkay, *Príspevok k poznaniu malých stredovekých opevnení na juhozápadnom Slovensku,* 258–259.

11th century. The court was situated on a gentle slope which is protected on one side by the edge of a swamp. From the fortifications remained only a channel and from residential buildings remained remnants of a brick building (10 x 6.5 meters) with shallow foundations and an oven in the corner. Remains of fortifications with residential buildings are in superposition with structures from the 9th to 11th centuries and discovered material dates back to the first half of the 12th and the first third of the 13th century.[88] In that century it was possible that nobles also built settlements on the upland promontory above Drážovce, where the Church of St. Michael is still standing. However, archaeological research has not yet confirmed this possibility.[89] The courts from the 11th–12th centuries may indirectly point to rural churches where the empora represented the allocated space for the landlord and his family. Because of this manorial courts are searched for close to this type of church.[90] So far, only in rare cases can the relationship between manor houses and churches be safely documented. These are settlements found in Partizánske-Šimonovany, Skalica and Nemešany-Zalužany. Most of the locations have no sacral buildings registered in their vicinity.[91] Certain indications exist in the locality Baratka near Levice where two Romanesque churches stood. Geophysical locality exploration has managed to locate remains of a larger building, probably from the Middle Ages.[92]

The large development of small minor nobility settlements in south-western Slovakia falls mainly in the 13th century. In that century occurred the massive construction of castles as a result of the devastating Tartar invasion. The manor house, together with the castle, comprised the complex defense system of the country and was a symbol of the social status of the

---

88 Ruttkay, Ruttkay and Šalkovský, *Slovensko vo včasnom stredoveku,* 146; Bazovský and Elschek, *Osídlenie v Bratislave-Dúbravke v 9. -13. storočí II. Stredoveký dvorec,* 85–96.

89 Ruttkay, *Sídla spoločenských elít na strednom Ponitrí v 9. - 13. Storočí,* 84.

90 Fiala, Habovštiak and Štefanovičová, *Opevnené sídliská z 10. - 13. storočia na Slovensku,* 439.

91 Ruttkay, *Príspevok k poznaniu malých stredovekých opevnení na juhozápadnom Slovensku,* 258.

92 Bešina, *Zaniknutý románsky kostol sv. Martina na Baratke pri Leviciach, návrh na prezentáciu,* 79.

owner. Unlike western Europe, the building of small medieval fortresses in southwestern Slovakia was less intense. A similar situation existed in what is present-day Hungary, which demonstrates that the socio-economic situation in Hungary in the 12th–15th century did not require the increased need of building settlements for the petty rural nobility.[93]

Medieval castles are now preserved only in a fragmentary form or completely destroyed by mining, landscape cultivation or modern development. Remains of the castles mostly take the form of a hill in the shape of a truncated cone with traces of the fortified line with a moat. The beginnings of construction of the castles date back to the second half of the 12th century. Their origin is specified by findings from archaeologically studied localities in Branč, Chotín, Kamenín, Malá Mača, Malé Kosihy, Nitra-Chrenová, Topoľčianky, Trakovice and Velčice.[94]

From the 11th century, medieval castles appeared across a relatively large area of central and western Europe. These castles with their small size and strategic location had a defensive function with only few defenders. In addition, they also performed a kind of psychological and symbolic role in society's perception of vassals.[95] Together with other settlements of the lower nobility, small castles are the largest group of fortified settlements in the framework of the Middle Ages. On the central part of the hill stood the tower, most often made of wood – in exceptional circumstances from stone. They were mostly on the top or to the backs of hills and promontories or on sand or loess dunes. The situation on the ground depended on the design of the fortifications.[96] Castles represent a less fortified residence of minor rural nobility located mostly outside the village on a natural or elevated position. Water castles in the plains protected natural and artificial waterways or ditches.[97] In addition to strategically located high-rise

---

93 Ruttkay, *Príspevok k poznaniu malých stredovekých opevnení na juhozápadnom Slovensku*, 260.
94 Jaššo, *Stredoveké hrádky na západnom Slovensku*, 123.
95 Jaššo, *Stredoveké hrádky na západnom Slovensku*, 125.
96 Fiala, Habovštiak and Štefanovičová, *Opevnené sídliská z 10. - 13. storočia na Slovensku*, 437.
97 Polla, Slivka and Vallašek, *K problematike výskumu hrádkov a hradov na Slovensku*, 361.

locations, the castles were built in the vicinity of watercourses which provided natural protection and drinking and process water.[98] In consideration of the reality that they were bound to medieval surroundings, they couldn't be located in very remote places. Owners of the castles had to supervise the work of vassals. By building mounds and ditches they were raising the defenses of selected positions. An elevated position is a large advantage in the protection of a fortification. In the lowland area, the construction was conditioned by an increase in defense by an artificially formed embankment. Lowland plains' disadvantages were compensated by using different natural phenomena, such as river meanders or elevated river terraces. On raised embankments in the shape of a truncated cone was the tower of a small castle. It was important that the heaped embankment remained compact and resisted erosion. J. Unger[99] found on the basis of research of mottes from the 13th century in South Moravia that the slopes were consolidated by pieces of moss placed on each other around the perimeter ridges. There was a continuous grass surface created to avoid potential landslide of the soil.[100]

A motte from the territory of Western Slovakia had under previous knowledge a circular or elliptical shape of embankment with a core diameter of 10 to 45 meters and an average height of 2 to 7 meters.[101]The artificially formed cores of castles rarely appeared in hilly areas. Castle cores were located inside the fortified area that protected the fortification or they were separated by a ditch from their own bailey. Castles built in hard-to-reach places were protected by dry moat at the place of easiest access.

However, the question is why in strategic and difficult terrain they increased the size of the cores of castles. F. Jasso presents as a possible explanation, the military defense function of the embankment. The artificial upslope of the core prevented the use of some mining equipment, such as burning carts or rams. The structure of a wooden castle's tower could be relatively safe from ignition.

---

98   Jaššo, *Stredoveké hrádky na západnom Slovensku*, 126.
99   Unger, *Zpevňování svahů u opevněných objektů jižní Moravy 13.století*, 525.
100 Unger, *Zpevňování svahů u opevněných objektů jižní Moravy 13. století*, 525.
101 Jaššo, *Stredoveké hrádky na západnom Slovensku*,133–136.

Castles on a hill or promontory without artificial raising of surfaces represented a numerous and diverse group. This phenomenon was a result of the very rugged topography of Slovakia. Builders of castles adapted fortifications to the most efficient use of natural areas. Very often old fortifications from prehistoric times or from the early Middle Ages were used, but not the entire surface of a former fort, only the top part. According to current knowledge the sides of hilltops were often used and also their promontory extensions. As well as promontory positions, builders also used the side of small hills which permitted the enlargement of the fortified area protected by a mound and dry moat.

The heyday of medieval castles dates back to the 13th and 14th centuries. Current research does not determine the start of construction of castles in Slovakia. The results of research in neighboring countries state that castles date back to the 12th century, more precisely, in the second half of the century. Findings from Slovakia that date castles back to the 10th–11th century are still archeologically insufficiently substantiated. In written sources the minor nobility is mentioned sporadically from the 11th century, of which it can be deduced that the start of castle construction dates back at least to the 11th century. It should be borne in mind that castles of the motte type in the period before the 12th century did not appear in Slovakia. A less frequent occurrence of mottes is observed in the territory of modern Hungary, and in eastern Europe they are almost completely absent. For now, it remains questionable in what context they came to our territory, and without comprehensive research that cannot be answered. Another, perhaps local reason is based on the fact that many castles were in natural elevated positions fortified with mounds and without an artificially raised central ridge. In this case the possibility might be considered that these castles were created by simplifying and reducing the major tribal or indigenous princes' fortified settlements. The question of their gradual decline is unresolved. In terms of material artifacts obtained around these fortifications, it is clear that the youngest findings from the 15th and 16th centuries bear witnesses to a gradual extinction sometime in the 16th century. The gradual disappearance of castles could have been caused by the new economic and social situation and innovation of architectural fortification of facilities as a result of the development of military technology.[102] One possible cause of the castle's end was also the increasing demands of nobility for housing.

Manor houses and palaces provide more comfortable and more spacious housing, unlike castles where housing was much smaller. In the 1540s and 1560s, castles were still used by bands of Hussites.[103] During the 15th century, in connection with the orders of the sovereign, several castles were demolished in order to not fall into the hands of insurgents.[104]

---

102 Habovštiak, *Stredoveké hrádky na Slovensku*, 8.
103 Jaššo, *Stredoveké hrádky na západnom Slovensku*, 137.
104 Polla, Slivka and Vallašek, *K problematike výskumu hrádkov a hradov na Slovensku*, 362.

Viktória Bíziková

The importance of cultural heritage in education

(In upper secondary education with a focus on tourism)

Abstract: Cultural heritage demonstrates the development of society; it is the essence of the individual, regional and national identity and collective memory. In order to recover the contents of cultural heritage, it needs to be integrated into the existing society (not only) through the educational process. The usage of cultural heritage in the context of education is the current requirement of teaching cultural heritage to the younger generation. In our article, we emphasize the importance of cultural heritage in terms of its educational function.

Keywords: Cultural heritage, education, cultural education, cultural competence, educational process

Cultural heritage is an irreplaceable asset for a society. Discovering, exploring and assessing the significance of various objects of cultural heritage is conducted consciously and unconsciously in different situations, in different social groupings and by the individual, at all levels – local, sub-regional, regional, continental and global. In its broadest conception, it includes the cultural heritage of the Earth its memory and history from the beginning to the present in the form of tangible or intangible, animate and inanimate.[1]

The issue of cultural heritage is currently the subject of research of multiple disciplines, including ethnology, cultural studies, museology, tourism

---

1   Johnová, *Marketing kulturního dědictví a umění*, 31.

and others. The variety of fields in the study of cultural heritage highlights the need for an interdisciplinary approach.

The intention of our article is to consider cultural heritage in the context of education and address cultural heritage from the perspective of its educational function. The thematic conception of the article requires research in cultural-educational terms.

It also reflects the current increasing interest in the cultural values of past generations, whose importance is increasing as a result of the global activities of many institutions. Regarding the importance of cultural heritage and its usage in the education of the younger generation, the object of interest here is presented as a value, form of knowledge, educational tool in shaping identity, a means of cultural reproduction and a significant factor in ensuring cultural continuity.

The importance of cultural heritage in education is evident in the content of numerous current policy documents and pieces of legislation at national, European and even global level. Their aim is, in a sustainable way, to systematically involve young people in the process of the protection and enhancement of cultural heritage through targeted education in this area.

The article is based on the principle of implementation of knowledge on cultural heritage in the process of teaching, in order to improve the application of culture in the educational and upbringing process in formal (institutionalized) education. The focus on the importance of cultural heritage in education also reflects the priorities and actions manifested in the policy document *Development Strategy of Culture for the Years 2014–2020*, which aims to build a cultural need and demand for culture through education.

In the article, we concentrate on the upper secondary education of the current educational system in the Slovak Republic with a focus on tourism, which provides vocational education and training for professionals working in tourism, the hotel industry in management positions of first contact with customers and front line management. The starting point is the theoretical intersections of three spheres – cultural heritage, tourism and education.

Objectives and methodology

The review article suggests that the role of an advanced knowledge society is[2] to promote awareness of cultural heritage, ensure cultural continuity and build the cultural identity of the younger generation, through the educational system.

The aim of the study is to concentrate on a new theoretical approach via a reflection on the parallels and interactions of culture, cultural heritage and education. It also analyzes the current legislative and policy support of the usage of cultural heritage in education and highlights selected aspects of cultural education.

The aim of the review article is to analyze the content and scope of the usage of cultural heritage in formal education in existing educational programs in upper secondary education with a focus on tourism. Within the methodology, we apply the elements of cultural heritage in teaching technical subjects in the example of the chosen field of study: hotel management.

As a part of the research problem, we seek answers to the following questions: What is the connection between cultural heritage, tourism and secondary vocational education with a focus on tourism? Is it important and necessary to use cultural heritage in the educational programs of fields of study with a focus on tourism? What is the current status of the usage of cultural heritage in the content of existing educational programs and what factors affect it? Is it possible to optimize the usage of cultural heritage in the content of educational programs?

In this article we apply the method of desk study, which is aimed at the exploration of cultural studies and available educational literature. A practical pedagogical study was conducted using the method of action research, oriented toward reflections of our own professional and pedagogical experience and solutions for technical-methodical problems of teaching. A supporting method is the content analysis of valid curricular documents.

---

2   In this paper, we use the term in the strict sense of the word, i.e., it includes only education and the school system.

List of key sources to research problems

In Slovakia, enough quality-processed and content-exhaustive literature and sources on culture, cultural heritage and its individual components are currently available. However, the importance of cultural heritage in education is a more closely specified area of scientific research and social discourse. Today there is an absence of a comprehensive look at this definition of the subject. In a review of key works and supporting studies, we present those in which the Slovak and foreign authors directly and indirectly engaged in the specified topic in different contexts.

In a wider context, we find the theoretical reflection of culture and learning to culture in culturological and anthropological works of the foreign authors V. Soukup (*Dějiny antropologie*), T. Edwards (*Kulturální teórie, klasické a současné přístupy*), C. Geertz (*Interpretace kultur*) and R. Lawless (*Co je kultura*), who in selected chapters outline various relational structures of culture and education. The conceptual apparatus that serves as a basis for the interpretation of the terminology frequently used is defined by Ch. Barker (*Slovník kulturálních studií*). Barbara Putz-Plecko at the University of Applied Arts in Vienna implements foreign research activities in the field of cultural education. In her review articles, she publishes work on cultural education, promotion of cultural knowledge, creativity and the need for intercultural understanding through education.

Prominent national experts and authors of the specific context of culture and cultural heritage are J. Čukan, L. Lenovský, B. Michalik, M. Dubská, M. Sopoliga, J. Botík and others. Frequently asked questions on culture and cultural heritage in relation to areas such as management, marketing, geography and tourism are broached by, e.g., J. Kredatus, J. Klinda, R. Johnová, M. Tajtáková, L. Kesner, J. Strelková, H. Pravdová, A. Plencner, V. Dolinská, A. Lašáková, K. Bartová, M. Lačný, Ľ. Kmeco, S. Benčič, I. Chorvát, Z. Profantová, P. Chrastina and others.

Work on the cooperation between cultural studies and education can be found in the academic writings of V. Gažová (*Perspektívy kulturológie, Úvod do kulturológie*). She presents an informed opinion on the current issues, concepts and perspectives of cultural education, the need for cultural education and the formation of cultural competencies which are necessary for the life of an individual in a globalized society.

The basis of the anthropological background of education in cultural and historical context is explained by B. Malík (*Pedagogická antropológia.*).

Another important approach enriching the cultural context, cultural heritage and education is answering the questions of the usage of art and culture in education through specific school subjects. The implementation of culture and arts into education through art is described by B.Šupšáková (the project *Art and Media in Education*), through ethics by A. Fischer, through music by J. Veres and through multicultural education by E. Mistrík, who is also the author of the teaching materials *Kultúra a multikultúrna výchova*, methodical manuals *Multikulti na školách* for the school subject of the same name and also a book *Základy estetiky a etikety, Umenie a kultúra* for the first, second and third grades of grammar school. He explains different cultures and the multicultural context, including the use of cultural heritage in education, and provides guidance on the implementation of cultural education in view of the requirements of the state's education policy. S. Kopčáková and E. Kušnírová deal with the protection of cultural heritage as a problem of the curricular field and school subject Art and Culture. Analysis of the specifics of multiculturalism and education is dealt with by V. Cabanová, I. Kominarec and E. Kominarecová. The authors mentioned above emphasize the need for changes not only in the school curriculum but in all learning environments with a view to applying elements of culture, arts and cultural heritage.

Comprehensive analysis including comparative information in the field of cultural and artistic education is provided by the publication EACEA, *Eurydice Arts and Cultural Education at Schools in Europe*, which assesses the state of art education in the curriculum in 30 European countries, including Slovakia.

Interdisciplinary communication in the social sciences with an emphasis on the educational potential of art and culture is supported by the online magazine *Culture, Arts and Education* by the Faculty of Education at Palacky University in Olomouc. The articles of various authors reflect the broad anthropological, cultural and social links between the arts and education and the other material and spiritual values of mankind. An important source of culturological overview is the volumes of *Acta Culturologica* from the Department of Culture, Faculty of Arts, at Comenius University in Bratislava. The results of the current research activities of the young generation at the Cultural Studies Department feature in the electronic scientific journal *Motus in Verbo* published by the Faculty of Arts, Matej Bel University. In the scientific periodical *Contexts of Culture and Tourism*, edited at the Department of Culture and Tourism Management at the Faculty of Arts at the University of Constantine the Philosopher in Nitra, various theoretical reflections of culture, cultural heritage and tourism are presented.

A major source is an extensive publishing database in educological sciences, which we apply in the context of the importance and usage of cultural heritage in education.

The terminology of educational sciences at the international level comes from TESE: the *Thesaurus for Education Systems in Europe*. We also used a thesaurus for education systems in the Czech Republic. Databases are processed and published by the Agency for Education, Audiovisual and Culture, EACEA; through its programs it coordinates Arts and Cultural Education at schools in Europe and calls for the development of cultural competence by education at schools.

Among the contemporary Slovak and Czech authors and experts in the specific context of education in the context of defining topic, we include J. Průcha L. Zormanová, E. Walter, J. Mares, P. Stech, M. Burin, J. Manak, I. Turek, V. Svec, T. Janik, M. Zelina, V. Rosa, B. Pupala, O. Kaščák, P. Kmet, Ľ. Višňovský, V. Kačáni, S. Hlásna, D. Čábalová, E. Petlák, R. Šlosár, J. Duchovičová, V. Kurincová, G. Petrova, J. Novák, A. Gogová, Š. Kročková, G. Pintes and I. Konečná Veverková.

Directly and indirectly, theoretically or applied, some technical studies published in educational journals of domestic and foreign origin are dedicated to our topic. They are *European Education*, *European Educational Research Journal*, *European Journal of Education*, *Educational Review*, *Pedagogika.sk*, *Pedagogické rozhľady*, *Pedagogická revue*, *Technológia vzdelávania*, *Pedagogické spektrum*, *Učiteľské noviny* and *či Didaktika*. A valuable source of information about what is happening in education is the documentation on education – about the real state of the educational system in Slovakia – that provides data as standard and non-standard outputs from the various available databases.

The importance of cultural heritage in education aids and emphasizes also various methodological recommendations, conventions and declarations, which we synthesize in a separate report.

Terminological and theoretical definition of the issue

The clear and precise technical definitions of the review article are influenced by its terminological and theoretical basis. Within them, we show the mutual relations and define the meaning of key terms.

Culture and education represent an area of special human activity. Their social and spatiotemporal specification represents phenomena and processes that are present throughout human existence. Humans, due to their specific make up, are entirely dependent on and anthropologically adapted to culture and education. For centuries, the genus Homo has been developing and progressing through the creativity of the human spirit and the ability of education as a lifelong process. Culture as a very complex and multifaceted phenomenon is an integral part of educational reality.

The culture represents not only the accumulated, inherited and adapted results of human activity, the experience, knowledge, attitudes, beliefs, explanations, ideas, desires, visions and successes, but also failures, sins, missteps and mistakes of previous generations. We can call the concept of cultural heritage a sort of biography of society and its culture, global and local, that which is the most valuable, characteristic and constitutional.[3]

We significantly apply the definition of heritage given by law. The Declaration by the Slovak National Council on the protection of cultural heritage adopted on February 28, 2001 (Journal of Laws of the Slovak Republic no. 91/2001, Coll. 39 of March 20, 2001) states that the cultural heritage of the Slovak Republic is *"the irreplaceable wealth of the state and its citizens, it is evidence of developed society, philosophy, religion, science, art, the document of educational and cultural level of the Slovak nation, other nations, minorities, ethnic groups and individuals who live or previously lived in Slovakia. Individual types and parts of cultural heritage are equal and they form an integral part of the cultural heritage of Europe and of all mankind."*[4]

---

3   Lenovský, *Cestovný ruch a kultúrne dedičstvo*, 100.
4   *NC SR Declaration on the Protection of Cultural Heritage 91/2001.*

It includes architectural, archaeological, intellectual, historical, artistic, technical, documentary and esthetic values. The content of cultural heritage is not only registered, legislative and institutionally protected, but also that which is undocumented and unclassified, and even that which is undiscovered and unknown. Cultural heritage develops; it changes in time and space, accepts and creates new content. No element, phenomenon or source constitutes cultural heritage from the beginning of its existence, but in certain circumstances, for example, in changing socio-cultural and socio-economic conditions, may (or may not) become so. Cultural heritage can be classified in several ways, for example, by nature, location, age and period, ownership, management, type or status quo.[5]

In our environment, the classification of cultural heritage came from the declaration of the National Council of the Slovak Republic (NR SR). It has distinguished immaterial (spiritual) cultural heritage and material (tangible) cultural heritage as follows: *"Cultural heritage is tangible and intangible values, movable and immovable property, including imported works and ideas that found a place and application in Slovakia. The immaterial value of cultural heritage is mainly oral and literal performances spread orally or by audio media, they are works of drama, music and dance art, customs and traditions, historical events, geographical, cadastral and local names."*[6]

The object of this study is the importance of cultural heritage in the context of education. The article uses the basic international concept of educological science education and understands it also in the Slovak context as "education in the broadest sense", an umbrella term for two parallel processes – education and upbringing, which are inextricably linked to the development of personality. This is a deliberate, systematic process of action for the individual's personality to develop in a positive sense its psychological features, functions and processes.[7]

An integral part of a developed, prosperous and educated society is a compact system of general and specific knowledge, which is represented by

5   Dubská, *Kultúrne dedičstvo a kultúrny cestovný ruch*, 16.
6   *NC SR Declaration on the Protection of Cultural Heritage 91/2001.*
7   Duchovičová and Kurincová at al., *Teoretické základy výchovy a vzdelávania*, 19–20.

knowledge as a source of the cultural identity, creativity and humanity of an individual as a member of society and representative of contemporary civilization. The dynamics of socio-cultural processes in the 21st century undoubtedly mean that there are constant changes in the requirements of the cultural competence of an individual.[8] An adequate response is cultural education through the development of cultural competencies, throughout the whole schooling of the individual. Cultural education should (must) be presented not only in every aspect of educational activity, but also integrated into education and training through educational objectives – key competencies.[9]

Changes in the world indicate a tendency that society will be increasingly integrated and globalized. At the same time there is an effort to find mechanisms for the maintenance of inherent (national, cultural) identity. Bringing together different cultures is rewarding when individuals are able to maintain their identity and respect the identity of other ethnic, cultural, linguistic and religious societies. The discussed phenomenon generates and provides a space for cultural education, whose task is to drag the individual in to his own culture and at the same time to implant tolerance and empathy of foreign cultures. Key instruments widely defined by the culture of education are culture and art.

The term cultural education is significantly understood as identical to its conceptual equivalents – culture, education by culture, cultural and artistic education.

From a comprehensive set of competencies, some are defined and developed through school education, the so-called key competencies, which are useful in most professions, and enable an individual to successfully cope

---

8   Gažová, *Perspektívny kulturológie.Modely kultúrnej výchovy na prelome tisícročí*, 202.
9   The list of key competencies by the EP and Council of December 18, 2006, on key competencies for lifelong education are: 1. Communication in the mother tongue, 2. Communication in foreign languages, 3. Mathematical competence and basic competencies in science and technology, 4. Digital competence, 5. Learning to learn, 6. Social and civic competencies, 7. Sense of initiative and entrepreneurship and 8. Cultural awareness and expression (Turek, *Didaktika*, 208–214).

with rapid changes in working, personal and social life. Cultural education is closely related to targets named *cultural awareness and expression*, the so-called cultural competencies.

Cultural competence represents an understanding of the importance of the creative expression of ideas, experiences and emotions through the media, including music, performing arts, literature and fine arts. Essential knowledge, skills and attitudes related to this competence are the knowledge of the culture including an awareness of local, national and European cultural heritages, and their place in the world. It covers a basic knowledge of major cultural works, including folk culture. Competence supports the understanding of linguistic and cultural diversity in Europe and other regions of the world, the meaning of esthetic factors in everyday life. Cultural skills relate to both appreciation and expression of awareness and enjoyment of works of art. They also include the development of creativity, artistic expression and the understanding of the economic and social opportunities of cultural activities. Cultural expression is the basis of creative skills, which can be converted into professional skills. It promotes the knowledge of one's own identity and culture as the basis for an open attitude and respect in relation to the diversity of cultural expression. A positive attitude also covers creativity and the willingness to cultivate esthetic capacity through artistic self-expression and ideas through participation in cultural life.[10]

Legislative and policy support for the usage of cultural heritage in education

The role of a developed society is to protect, cultivate, restore, access and present the cultural potential, cultural values and heritage of the country in a sustainable manner. This role, and many related ones, is contained in documents applicable at a national, European and even global level. The key starting point for the implementation of the mentioned tasks is to systematically involve young people in the process through targeted education in this area.

---

10 Turek, *Didaktika*, 214.

The promotion of this education policy is built into the mechanisms of legislative and policy documentation supporting the implementation of the general objectives of cultural education in society.

Important international documents for such purposes include, the Convention for the Protection of the World Cultural and Natural Heritage UNESCO (1972), ratified by the Slovak Republic in 1993. In Chapter VI on education programs, Article 27 of the convention states that *"Member States shall endeavour by all appropriate means particularly through educational and information programmes to ensure that their nations value and respect increasingly cultural and natural heritage."*[11]

The role of cultural and artistic education, by forming competencies for young people's lives in the 21st century, has been widely recognized at the European level. In 1995, the Council of Europe, COE, launched a major project focusing on culture, creativity and youth. The project examined the existing arts education in schools of member states, as well as the involvement of professional artists and the availability of extra-curricular activities. The result was a survey of arts education in Europe and an international colloquium.

In 2005, the Council of Europe initiated the frame work *Convention about the Value of Cultural Heritage for Society*, which identified the need for European countries to preserve cultural resources, promote cultural identity, respect diversity and promote intercultural dialogue. Article 13 of the framework acknowledged the important place of cultural heritage within arts education but also recommended developing linkages between courses in different fields of study.

In 2008, the Council published a white paper on intercultural dialogue, which offered an intercultural approach to managing cultural differences. The paper identified educational organizations (including museums, heritage sites, kindergartens and schools) that have the potential to support intercultural exchange, learning and dialogue through arts and cultural activities.

Important policy documents of the European Union (EU), stressing the need of education, include the *Sorbonne Declaration, Bologna Declaration,*

---

11 *Convention for the Protection of the World Cultural and Natural Heritage.*

the Memorandum on Lifelong Learning and the *Copenhagen Declaration* on enhanced European cooperation in technical education and training.[12]

A minor development toward promoting a cultural policy of education has arisen in the context of the European Union. The European Commission proposed a *European Agenda for Culture*, approved by the Council of the European Union in 2007. This Agenda acknowledges the value of arts education in developing creativity. The strategic framework for European cooperation in education and training over the next decade clearly emphasizes the importance of transversal key competencies, including cultural awareness and creativity.[13]

Culture as a part of education is supported by *The recommendations of the European Parliament and the Council from 18th December 2006 about the key competences for lifelong learning*; under it the Member States of the European Union should develop in schools of all types, including lifelong-learning ones, a national system of education core competences, among which are highlighted "cultural competencies".

Besides these major developments in international and European cooperation, there have been a number of conferences and activities, some of which have led to changes in the concept of artistic and cultural education. An example is the international conference on the promotion of cultural education in Europe – Promoting Cultural Education in Europe (Austrian Presidency of the EU 2006). The meeting of representatives of the European network of state workers of arts and cultural education – *European Network of Civil Servants Working in the Field of Arts and Cultural Education* – was very important because it aimed to create a general basis for defining cultural education and create the dictionary *European Glossary on Arts and Cultural Education*.

In 2007, the Commission presented a communication on a European agenda for culture in a globalizing world – the *Communication on a European agenda for culture in a Globalising World*. The answer took the form of a Council Resolution: *Council on a European Agenda for Culture* from 2007 recommended encouraging art education and active participation in cultural activities to develop creativity and innovation.

---

12 Belovič, *Hlavné dokumenty EÚ v oblasti vzdelávania*, 2–4.
13 *Arts and Cultural Education at School in Europe.*

The resolution was followed by a work plan for culture – *Work Plan for Culture 2008–2010*. The Commission recognized the importance of culture and creativity by designating the year 2008 as the European Year of Intercultural Dialogue, and the year 2009 as the Year of Creativity and Innovation.

In the legal system of the Slovak Republic, the constitution supports the preservation of cultural heritage. An important legal document related to the issue of promoting cultural education for us is the Declaration of the Slovak National Council for the Protection of Cultural Heritage (2001). Article No 6 of the Declaration states that *"the government will create conditions for school and after-school education and the strengthening of relations of cultural heritage, especially among the younger generation."*[14]

Principles and criteria of sustainability and sustainable development with an emphasis on long-term processes and synergy effects are manifested in the *National Strategy for Sustainable Development of the Slovak Republic*. In addition to political, legal, economic and organizational tools, the document requires the participation and cooperation of educational tools for supporting value orientation, cultural production, determining values and heritage protection. Ideas of TUR or selected parts of local and regional *Agenda 21* are applicable not only in dozens of villages, towns and companies, but are gradually entering into teaching at universities, and secondary and primary schools.[15]

The promotion of culture through education and training within the broader context is expressed in *the strategy for cultural development of the Slovak Republic for 2014–2020* published by the Ministry of Culture. It analyzes the current state of culture in Slovakia, its status, strengths and weaknesses, etc. Mentioned in the list of weaknesses is that the *"low demand for culture is directly related to the lack of formation of cultural needs, whether due to the action of the media, but the most important role here is played by a low emphasis on education in culture within the educational process."*[16] Under the proposed priorities and measures within the

---

14 NC SR *Declaration on the Protection of Cultural Heritage 91/2001*.
15 *National Strategy for Sustainable Development*.
16 *Development Strategy of Culture of the Slovak Republic for 2014–2020*.

content of this document is formed a strategic area of cultural needs and demand for culture and education.

The main vision for better application of culture in education is contained in the documents: *The concepts of the development of local and regional culture, Concept for traditional culture* and *Development strategy of local and regional culture.*

In the area of school legislation, the importance of cultural heritage in education is supported by Act. 245/2008 Coll. *on Education and upbringing (School Act) and on amendments to certain laws,* which in § 4 of the goals of education in letter f) states *"…to strengthen the respect of parents and other persons towards the cultural and national values and traditions of the State of which they are citizens, towards the state language, their mother tongue and towards their own culture."*[17]

Education as one of the enduring priorities and features of the long-term perspective of society is declared by the Government Policy Statement from the year 1998 – *National Programme of Education in the Slovak Republic for the next 15–20 years* (Millennium).

A comprehensive program of objectives, solutions, content, methods and forms of educational process, strategies and methods of evaluation, organization and management of education is presented in an educational programme called curriculum. It is one of the most important pedagogical documents for different types of schools and also for specific schools. In line with current trends in the countries of the EU and the OECD, in our country a two-level curriculum model has been established in the form of a state and school curriculum.

The ultimate and binding document, setting out the general objectives of education and core competencies (including cultural), is the State Curriculum (SC) as Level I of the two-tier program system of education in our country. Educational objectives are created to ensure the balanced development of the personality of students. The SC defined for different levels of education and fields of education forms the compulsory frame-work of state-guaranteed education. It sets out the basic target requirements for the competence of graduates and the derived performance and content

---

17 The Education Act. Z.z 245/2008.

standards of general and professional components of education, graduate profile, educational areas, cross-cutting topics, a framework of teaching plans and the framework curriculum, conditions for implementing the program, including the characteristics of the conditions for the development of students with special educational needs. It is the basis for the development of the school education program, which takes into account the specific conditions and needs of the region. The state curriculum is issued and published for individual levels of education by the Ministry of Education, Science, Research and Sport of the Slovak Republic. The State Educational Institute, the National Institute of Technical Education, the Research Institute of Child Psychology and Psychology in Bratislava and expert commissions with a team of selected teachers for individual subjects are involved in the development process of the State Curriculum. A significant change in the educational policies of schools in legislative, educational, social and evaluative terms is represented by Level II of the program system – the School Education Program (hereinafter SEP). It's an important curricular educational document with optional content in education at teaching plan level, strengthening school autonomy and responsibility for their processing and quality. Schools can create an SEP according to the goals and needs of the region. It is a document containing organized school activities, learning objectives and the content of teaching and learning outcomes. SEPs are governed by CS requirements. An SEP is developed by supplementing the CS with specific needs on the basis of proposals and needs of regions, companies, parents, students and other stakeholders. It must ensure compliance with local labor market needs with the active participation of employers at the regional or local level, increasing the requirement for better employment and job opportunities for graduates of schools.[18]

18 Curricular transformation and new possibilities for the application of traditional and folk culture in the curriculum of primary schools in 2012 prompted the formation of a civic association called the Association of Teachers of Schools with Regional Education based in Slovenská Ľupča. Members of the association are schools that within the SEP have created a subject in regional education ("Association of Teachers from Schools with Regional Education.").

The defined general and framework (partial) objectives of education, upbringing and core competencies are in educational practice specified and developed in stages into specific objectives contained in the curriculum.[19]

Cultural education at the level of a particular teaching unit in the context of the program is contained in the microstructure of the curriculum in the form of *Written preparation for teaching*, which includes didactic analysis of the curriculum (subject-matter). In its content the teacher transforms the knowledge of the scientific system into a didactic system with an emphasis on educational value while respecting didactic objectives and principles. Particularly, in shaping and developing cultural competence, emphasis is placed not only on the reporting function concentrated on knowledge about culture and cultural heritage, but especially on the formative function focused on growth of the relationship to values and development of character and the volitional, moral, esthetic, emotional and other attitudes and characteristics of individual personalities influencing and directed toward socially desirable outcomes.

The importance of cultural heritage in education

One of the main tasks of school education is, in a socially desirable manner, to shape a student's personality, allowing them to grow into their own culture through the process of enculturation and comprehensively prepare them for work, private and public life with adequate cultural facilities such as cultural literacy in society.

Cultural heritage is an important and indispensable part of cultural education. The Slovak Republic has undertaken to abide by the principles enshrined in the already mentioned legal and policy documents, treaties, conventions and recommendations by various institutions on the use of cultural heritage in the national educational system.

Cultural heritage is a source of historical knowledge, documents, memory and developments of a particular nation, other nations, national minorities, ethnic groups and individuals. As a partial cross-sectional

---

19 Individually, in terms of curriculum, each teacher can prepare a teaching plan which is currently not prescribed as school pedagogical documentation.

feature of the curriculum, the topics it covers are didactic in meaning, function and purpose.

Representation and usage of cultural heritage in the education of the younger generation at every level of education according to the school system in Slovakia have important resonance arising from the requirements to protect and enhance the cultural values of previous generations. However, these requirements are predicated on knowledge of cultural heritage, building and developing the relationship to the cultural heritage of their own community, city, region and state. They form an integral part of the cultural heritage of Europe and the world, which corresponds to a globally oriented and pro-European dimension of education.

The body of knowledge on cultural heritage and our relationship with it can be in the future one of the key factors guaranteeing the survival of national and cultural identity in a globalizing, commercializing and informatizing world. The verdict of culturologist D. Hajek points to that link and we can agree, that *"in a period claiming globalization, or even just during this period, the importance of the existence of national cultures in the preservation and development of cultural heritage and humanization of society is increasing."*[20]

The importance of cultural heritage in education is also emphasized by the development strategy for culture in the Slovak Republic for the years 2014–2020. It characterizes cultural heritage as a perspective cultural sector not only with social value but also with economic potential and it further states that *"if we want to increase the demand of the population for cultural activities, we have to begin with education. In the educational process it is necessary to create instruments which can awaken awareness of cultural needs in students. Cultural education and training should greatly contribute to the growth of interest in culture in Slovak society."*[21]

The usage of cultural heritage in education is also important in terms of multiculturalism. Multicultural education as a sub-topic can be part of any school subject, or may be formed in the curriculum as a separate subject. Through knowledge of their own cultural heritage, through knowledge of "others" and through knowledge of the world (as a collection of

20 Hajko, *Globalizácia a kultúrna identita*, 77.
21 *Development Strategy of Culture of the Slovak Republic for 2014–2020.*

different cultures)[22] in the context of cultural diversity, cultural differences (rather than irregularities), the younger generation can learn to identify the conflicts and coexistence of many cultures side by side as an essential/ natural reality.

The use of cultural heritage in the educational process performs multiple functions. The informative (educational) function, which has a comprehensive and professional learning dimension, and the formative (upbringing) function, are both important in terms of the dichotomous division of objectives in the educational process.

The informative function is the acquisition of knowledge, skills and habits appropriate to the age of the students and relevant to the type of school and to the focus of the field of study. A part of the knowledge of cultural heritage has a universal character. All the students should be familiar with it and know it in the frame of key competencies and components of general education. As part of this, the general educational function of cultural heritage complements general knowledge that forms the necessary educational basis for all members of society and completes a relatively comprehensive picture of the knowledge of the world in a cultural context.

The technical learning function differs from the general function in the breadth and depth of acquiring knowledge, skills and habits, and the manner of their usage. Technical learning with deepened and expanded usage of cultural heritage is designed to prepare professionals with the performance of qualified work mainly in artistic, cultural, pedagogical and other related job positions, for example, in the tourism sector.

The formative function of the use of cultural heritage in education lies in educational activity developing and shaping the character, volitional, cognitive, intellectual, professional, moral, esthetic, emotional and other attitudes and properties of students. It influences the formation of required activation-motivation, relation-attitude, self-regulation and dynamic traits. Deliberate action is governed by conventional rules and its objectives are achieved in various ways, means and methods. The basic starting point of the formative function is value orientation. It has

---

22 Closer to the theoretical reflection on multiculturalism of Lenovský, *Kultúra kúpeľného mesta*, 153–168.

its axiological dimension, respecting the proven principles and practices generated by experience, the implementation of which contributes to the successful and efficient achievement of educational goals.[23]

A number of topics in the context of cultural heritage give space through the pedagogical activities in the students' education to a positive relationship with cultural heritage, esthetic sense, creativity and love of art, and to the respect for cultural values and diversity. This leads to respect for the legislation of the protection of cultural heritage, responsibility, thoughtfulness and to multicultural tolerance. The functions of the usage of cultural heritage in education cannot be implemented individually, but in dialectical unity. They are connected in the purposeful and systematic development of the pupil's personality to constant self-improvement and development of cognitive skills, including critical, rational and logical thinking, and creative abilities.

The aim of the use of cultural heritage in education is to recognize the tangible and intangible cultural heritage of the ancestors of one's native village, city, region and country, and to create conditions for the growth and development of the relationship to cultural values and to integrate them into the structure of the individual personality. In educational activities in order to benefit from cultural heritage it is necessary to focus attention not only on the native culture as a source of cultural identity, but also the recognition of cultural diversity and its richness. A generally formulated objective needs to be, of course, from the didactic point of view, concretized and specified into an elementary unit – a lesson with defined content and performance standards. In accordance with didactic principles, it is necessary for its teaching that the usage of the cultural heritage follow from native to foreign and from local to global.

Implementation of cultural heritage in the educational process is important not only in terms of sharing information on cultural heritage, and

---

23 In the educational sciences, access to culture and to its examination is different to most other sciences of culture. In contrast with cultural studies and anthropology, teachers do not consider all cultural products valuable (and educational) and worthy of the criterion of cultural quality. In this definition of culture, the axiological approach is expressed, which is the most preferred approach in relation to culture and education focused on the sphere of positive values.

cultivation and improvement of the individual, but especially in terms of the formation of a culturally competent generation assuming its cultural identity, which shows demand for cultural products and activities, and is ready to lead a life in a multicultural society.

The content of cultural heritage education can be identified in the educational program at particular levels and inter-levels of the Slovak school system, but with a different breadth and depth. What should be the optimal content and scope of the school curriculum in pedagogical theory is still considered a contradictory and unresolved question.

The usage of cultural heritage in the context of education and its particularities

In reviewing the use of cultural heritage in the context of education it is necessary to apply a theoretical basis of pedagogy and didactics. In view of the aforementioned disciplines within our research subject, we emphasize that cultural heritage is an integral part of cultural education primarily through institutionalized formal education in schools.

The use of cultural heritage in education supports the development of key competencies, mainly cultural (cultural awareness and expression), social and civic competencies. The use of cultural heritage in education performs a comprehensive and professional learning function, along with many others, for example socialization, enculturation, educational, preventive, therapeutic and so on.

It is an integral feature of the content of education in the areas of school educational programs and as a topic it is included in the content of compulsory subjects and optional subjects. Cultural heritage is applied in the educational program as a cross-cutting topic, especially in the context of multicultural education, regional education and traditional folk culture (especially in primary and secondary education), while according to the school profile, it can be the subject of a separate educational curriculum in the context of elective hours.

As a topic, cultural heritage can in an unlabored way be integrated into the teaching of any applicable subjects through their content and through different organizational forms (e.g. excursions, projects, classes, homework, after-school activities, training courses, work experience and others). At the same time cultural heritage in education creates and reinforces horizontal and vertical cross-curricular connections.

In the context of the usage of cultural heritage in education[24], it is possible to identify certain peculiarities from the didactic point of view, in addition to generally applicable elements,.

In general terms, the learning process involves: *learning* activity on the part of students, where the students acquire knowledge, skills and habits, develop their skills, shaping their attitudes, relationship to themselves, to other people, to the environment, life, world and so on; and *teaching* activities on the part of the teacher, i.e., the management process of cognitive and practical activities of students, management and shaping of their attitudes to life, the world etc., and management of their skills and their entire personality.[25]

Defining elements of the educational process are the subject matter as a system of knowledge and activities, where the learning objectives are specified as a condition to be achieved. The dynamic factor is teacher-student interaction through methodology, organizational forms and material means, whose choices are governed by didactic principles. In terms of other aspects of teaching, a great deal of research on communication, the teaching style of a teacher, school environment, social climate in the classroom and so on is currently available. The educational process with the usage of cultural heritage stems from the general regularities of the learning process that is examined by didactics.

At the same time the educational process represents the union of the informative and formative aspects. Neither of them can be underestimated nor overestimated. The use of cultural heritage in education does not necessarily have a tendency or effort to "teach students the most". In the context of the curriculum of cultural heritage, the teacher's educational impact cannot be substituted via quantity of transmitted information, as it does not lead automatically to the quality of the acquired knowledge,

---

24 Concepts to educate, school teaching, teaching process and educational process, are considered herein as synonyms.
25 Turek, *Didaktika*, 20.

skills and habits of students and unconditionally to the formation of cultural heritage.

The creation and shaping of a positive attitude toward material and spiritual cultural values is a process requiring the linking of emotions and experiences, leading from internal experience and admission to identification. To be closer to the target, it is necessary to overcome the traditional interpretative approach.

Based on personal experience, we believe that more important than rapidly dating knowledge transfer is a need to learn how to learn and learn for life. With the development of ICT communication, information has become readily available, and therefore it is not necessary to emphasize the acquisition of direct knowledge. The personal capacities and experience of students with cultural heritage are shifting to the center of attention, along with their access to knowledge and their personal and social competencies. The teaching process should be kept in a manner in which not only the teacher is active, but the activity is transferred to the student. A variety of innovative, activating, demonstrative and heuristic teaching methods that are interesting, beneficial and that help to arouse interest in cultural heritage are effective for this purpose. A natural expression of the formative relationship is if the interest in cultural heritage goes beyond the classroom and the school and influences the student in extracurricular time, during after-school activities, while doing their hobbies and living their lives.

To improve interactive communication among students and teachers it is effective to make cultural heritage more available in addition to modern methods and means of information technology and usage of available digital resources. A significant feature of the use of ICT in education is creating one's own materials as teaching aids. When creating teaching materials we must, of course, take into account the objective of lessons, the level at which students feel comfortable working with computers, the methods and tools of processing information students are familiar with, and how critically they can evaluate the available resources. The appropriate use of technical means provides better feedback, the curriculum is demonstrative, more accessible and, for students, more interesting.

Another important prerequisite to achieve the stated learning objectives is to bring closer the theory that is backed up by the latest research and examples of specific economic, cultural and social practice. In the context of the usage of cultural heritage, it is essential to bring real life together with school and when it is possible make use of examples of the near surroundings of the school in the direction from local to global.

A special feature of the educational process with usage of cultural heritage is interdependence and linking various subjects in one grade, both in general education and training, but also among different grades. Tight horizontal and vertical cross-curricular relations can be used by a teacher and applied in order to achieve comprehensive and conceptual thinking. The point is that students do not get isolated knowledge, skills and habits of cultural heritage from individual subjects, but they are able to apply them in solving various tasks and problems.

An essential requirement of teaching via the use of cultural heritage is an updated curriculum on the basis of the latest scientific knowledge and changes in political, economic, cultural and social areas in our country and around the world. In order to increase quality and efficiency, it is necessary that each teacher reflects their own level of preparation for teaching, and that they use proper didactic principles and select appropriate methods and tools. It is desirable to change the traditional roles and status of teachers to new roles, specifically in the eyes of students – those of coordinator, instructor, consultant, moderator and advisor. The new roles entail specific requirements that may be defined through professional, pedagogical and social skills.

Perhaps the most striking peculiarity of the teaching process in the usage of cultural heritage are the external and internal conditions as relevant circumstances in which this process occurs and which affects the teaching. An important role is played by external conditions: natural, social, historical, regional, local environment and so on. As regards the internal conditions of the teaching process aimed at the student, not only are the state of mental and physical development, existing knowledge, skills, habits, interests and personality traits important, but in the context of cultural heritage, the identity of the student and the reflection of their own cultural identity is especially salient.

Each student comes from their own unique culture, typical for the local community, and they identify themselves with their home culture. Based on a thorough knowledge of these conditions the teacher can significantly influence students' motivation, their personal interest in education and the relationship of students to cultural heritage as a priority in their close environment.

Finally, the teacher can, through this tool, significantly affect the environment and atmosphere in the classroom. Cultural heritage offers a variety of topics through which it is possible to convert formality to informality and sincere openness.

We especially emphasize that much of the mediated knowledge of cultural heritage especially at local and regional level is experienced by students emotionally and reviewed rationally because it is associated with a specific experience; self-consciousness is activated and self-image in the local community is portrayed. The usage of cultural heritage clearly helps to define and shape further awareness of the cultural identity of the student and also helps them to learn about their previously unrecognized cultural traditions.

If in the learning process in the context of cultural heritage there are properly submerged elements such as the environment that students come from, for example, rural, urban, metropolitan, agrarian, industrial and so on, and their identity, then it creates space for personal fulfillment, and communication occurs with a very rich cultural foundation rewarding all the students and also teachers. The mutual exchange of ideas, stories and information about cultural heritage are an enrichment which can be fully described as a "hidden curriculum" of teaching content as well as other specifics of the usage of cultural heritage in education.

The outlined particularities of the educational process with the usage of cultural heritage are an open list of specifics that can be continually updated based on the experience acquired during creative solutions to various methodological and technical problems and systematic reflection on teaching practice.

Upper secondary education with a focus on tourism

In the context of the usage of cultural heritage in upper secondary education with a focus on tourism, it is necessary to highlight the link and connections between *cultural heritage and tourism.*

Although cultural heritage is a part of tourism, it is obvious that not all of the volume of cultural heritage is linked to tourism.[26] As a cross-cutting topic, cultural heritage is a part of the creation of cultural competence and cultural education of students through school education. It is the most important factor in forming and maintaining cultural identity. The link with tourism is not only in the fact that cultural heritage is an important part of tourism and has economic value, but also in the fact that tourism is (or should be) one of the tools of its optimum utilization, protection and development. In today's multicultural and globalized world, cultural heritage is one of the tools that can fight homogenization, cultural imperialism and preserve self-identity.[27]

Upper secondary education, the USE, in accordance with Act no. 245/2008 Coll. on education and upbringing, is a secondary vocational education that a student can obtain by successful completion of the last year of their study during at least a four-year and a maximum five-year education program in secondary vocational schools, which is evaluated by school-leaving examination. According to the International Standard Classification of Education, it represents grade ISCED 3.

In the description of types of secondary school issued by the Notice of the Ministry of Education no. 282/2009 Coll. on secondary schools (according to which they are grammar schools), secondary vocational schools (SVSs) provide upbringing and education in the system of vocational education and conservatories. These schools not only prepare graduates for work, but also for continuation of their studies. Their curriculum is built on a higher level of education and ensures continuous transition to tertiary education.

In the context of the usage of cultural heritage in USE educational programs (ISCED 3A), we concentrate on departments with a focus on tourism. This group includes the fields: 6324 M Management of Regional Tourism, 6354 M 01 Services and Entrepreneurship (the Hotel Industry), 6355 M Services in Tourism and 6323 K Hotel Academy. These are courses with a graduation exam and which prepare graduates for the labor market

---

26 Closer to a premise of cultural heritage and tourism, Dubská, *Kultúrne dedičstvo a cestovný ruch*, 31–45.

27 Lenovský, *Cestovný ruch a kultúrne dedičstvo*, 113–114.

in tourism, the hotel industry and gastronomy, or for further study in the context of continuity of education.

Education in selected fields, with a focus on tourism is realized by the State Curriculum: 62 Economic Sciences, 63 and 64 Economics and Organization, Retail and Services I. and II., etc. in force since 2013. The educational program is based on a uniform scheme applicable for all departments of STS: the learning areas include general education (Language and Communication, Man and Nature, Man, Society and Values, Mathematics and Information Work, Health and Movement), vocational education and training (theoretical education, practical training), thematic courses (Protection of Life and Health Physical Educational Training Course).

In general education, the SC describes the use of cultural heritage in subjects under the curriculum framework as follows: Slovak Language and Literature, Foreign Languages, History, Geography, Civics and Ethical Education. Within the scope of these subjects the graduates of USE focusing on tourism obtain a general knowledge base in the context of cultural heritage.

In the component of vocational education and training of the SEP, there are common standards developed for all departments: 63 and 64 represent a uniform basis and so-called specific educational standards for study departments of 63 and 64. In accordance with them, schools are entitled to create their own curriculum subjects.

In the common educational standards for TEE for department groups teaching 63, there is no overt mention of "cultural heritage", only a latent one in the description of content and performance standards.

In specific educational standards TEE for department groups teaching 63, there is no overt mention of cultural heritage, there is only latent. It should be noted that the SC constitutes the minimum requirements of the curriculum for a department in the group in which the SVS can be further profiled in their own SEP.

Within the available lessons, schools are entitled to create an optional subject and to include it in the curriculum according to their own requirements. Such an approach allows a two-level model of educational-upbringing programs in the reform of the school education system. It is obvious, and it is also a finding of our analysis of the curriculum that the mandatory method of determining the content of education is being abolished, especially in the group of optional subjects. The school is therefore in this respect, autonomous and independent. However, the delegation has a greater responsibility. There can also arise the opposite situation, so a school "can" create a subject, but it also "does not have to", which, in the field of study with direct respect to cultural heritage can induce a state of insufficient training of students in this direction.

Precisely determining the content and extent of usage of cultural heritage in the context of subjects of different departments in USE with a focus on tourism at the level of state education programs is not currently possible. Each school that has set up a tourism-related department should be approached individually, after studying and analyzing the content of its own SEP.

Application of selected elements of cultural heritage in teaching specialized subjects in the field of hotel academy

The tourism sector in our country has undergone significant changes in the last decade. These changes require new and creative approaches to education and training for tourism professionals.

Based on the best examples of educational practice, we offer methodological suggestions using selected elements of cultural heritage in teaching vocational subjects at a hotel academy. It is obvious that within the curriculum in USE with a focus on tourism, and also due to the profile of the graduate, it is not possible to comprehensively cover the whole content of cultural heritage. We focus on prioritizing selected features of cultural heritage that are regarded as valuable in the tourism industry, which should, in a field with a focus on tourism, be implemented in the educational process in an appropriate and creative way.

A methodological suggestion optimizing the usage of cultural heritage in technical education with a focus on tourism is realized at the secondary vocational school of hotel services and business in Nové Zámky in the field of hotel academy, within a framework of active research.

Elaborated topics include educational standards, a methodological approach and evaluation of activities. They eschew traditional teaching and more widely apply approaches emphasizing the active learning of students, creativity, process of discovery and search, acquisition of knowledge on the basis of experience, emotion and experience in interaction with classmates and teachers.

The developed methodological suggestions lead students to independent working, constructive and conceptual thinking, creative self-realization and active learning. The selected approach overcomes formalism in their knowledge and thus contributes to closer contacts with the regional and national culture and its various elements.

Our approach allows students to gain deeper insight into problems and become designers of their own learning. Students learn to communicate and work in teams and are more flexible, use information technology and orient themselves in the scientific literature and other sources. Learning becomes a form of play and experience in creating identity, developing feelings of cultural value and a relationship to region and country. Students gradually investigate the fact that we are as a nation culturally and spiritually very rich.

Our own experience shows that even students with poor results acquire a lot of new knowledge, practical experience and work with enthusiasm via the described task on the development of cultural competencies. The teacher has more space for research and professional development by the realization of these activities in the development of their creative and authorial competence.

Examples of educational practice

Methodological suggestion no. 1

School subject: Hotel and Catering Management
Thematic unit: Gastro Management
Topic: History of Slovak cuisine
The lesson: The gastronomic tradition of my (selected) community
Grade: Fourth
The main objectives:

– **Cognitive:** students can describe local gastronomy, interpret it in relation to the history of Slovak cuisine.

- **Affective:** students shape and strengthen local identity and create a positive value orientation in relation to their own culture.

Aids: dictaphone, worksheet with standardized questions for interview respondents, encyclopedic dictionary of gastronomy, ethnographic atlas

Form of work: individual work, homework

Course content: to recognize local eating habits and traditions. The gastronomic heritage of ancestors. Interview.

Performance standard: Students can locate a source of information, formulate questions in a controlled interview, prepare a record of the culinary traditions of their communities and present them.

Methodical approach: Eating habits are a part of cultural heritage, which includes tangible and intangible values. As part of the traditional folk culture, their potential lies in the basic assumption of undistorted cultural awareness of individuals, and the resulting awareness of the whole of society. The knowledge of the culinary heritage of ancestors of native municipalities strengthens the chain of identity, building from the personal and local to the regional and national identity and toward the European.

The aim is to support students in learning about and describing the eating traditions that are known by their grandparents, great-grandparents or the oldest inhabitants of the municipality where the student comes from. The students' task is to consult informants and create a controlled interview with an older person about the habits of traditional eating. The subject of discussion is the traditional food and gastronomy of the municipality in the past, or preserved and unpreserved in their families and communities. Students in their work are recommended to use a dictaphone so they miss nothing. It is necessary to warn students that questions must be prepared in advance if they want to get interesting information. It is best to prepare open questions. A student should also explain the context for obtaining information and interpret it in relation to geographical conditions (what produce is offered by the surrounding countryside), ethnic and religious composition of the population of the village, social status and wealth, employment, contacts, culture (local customs, knowledge, recipes) and occasions (religious holidays, custom calendar, everyday meals, Lent meals, etc.).

The students' task is to reproduce and present the results of their independent work. It is necessary to emphasize to them that the collected evidence will be preserved for future generations. The most important part is the discussion and summary. In the evaluation, we will concentrate on fulfillment of the task and objectives in the description of local traditional eating habits, to increase the knowledge on local and regional culture in catering, and in particular whether the acquired knowledge could be used by the student in describing the national gastronomy of Slovakia and gastronomy of ethnic minorities living in our country.

Evaluation of activity: As students come from different towns and villages throughout the Nitra region, they enrich the local gastronomic traditions and peculiarities not only for themselves but also for their schoolmates to form a mosaic of regional culture of the Nitra region and Danube region. The activity deepens the relationship with their hometown and also teaches them about research work in the field, primarily about obtaining information and then processing and presenting it. The suggested task also creates a bridge from past to present, from traditional eating habits to modern culinary trends, from knowledge of the native to knowledge of the foreign.

Methodological suggestion no. 2

School subject: Hotel and Catering Management
Thematic unit: Hotel industry as a part of tourism
Topic: Hotel industry in Slovakia
The lesson: The setting up of a property
Grade: Fifth
The main objectives:

- **Cognitive**: the student is able to describe the setting up of a traditional property in our country under the existing legislation, using elements of folk architecture.
- **Affective**: the student strengthens cultural identity and develops relationships with ethno-cultural traditions of Slovakia.

Tools: Edict MH SR no. 277/2008 "Laying down the classification signs for their division into categories and classes"; Ethnographic Atlas of Slovakia, PC, internet.

Form of work: group work, project

Time: 2 lessons

Other recommendations: draw lots for particular regions of Slovakia

Course content: describe the process of setting up the property, design of equipment, accessories and furniture.

Performance standard: The student is able to design and set up a property in traditional style (under current law) and to apply elements of folk architecture according to the characteristics of lowland, mountain and foothill region.

Methodological approach: The students' task is to design and establish a property as required by the category and class of the current legislation and to incorporate elements of traditional architecture as the most significant manifestation of the material culture of Slovakia. They use the Ethnographic Atlas of Slovakia and with its help they obtain information about the characteristics of lowland, mountain and foothill types of region, taking into account the functional and spatial characteristics of accommodation. The recommended properties to design are, e.g., a koliba (cottage house), guest house, barrelhouse and so on, with the relevant architectural, material and design elements of the selected region. It includes equipment design, product design, inventory, personnel clothing (costume) respecting the characteristics of the region in the context of its traditional style. A drawing is welcomed. A student argues by use of acquired knowledge from Geography in Tourism, other technical subjects and the Ethnographic Atlas of Slovakia. The task is time-consuming; it can be approached and evaluated as a project. Of course, there are consultations.

Evaluation activities: the task is to develop cultural competencies oriented toward ethno-cultural tradition in the material and technical culture of Slovak rural areas applied to the hotel industry. It emphasizes knowledge of the culture of Slovak regions in the course of business in the study field. The activity is one example of the use of cultural heritage in teaching technical subjects. It supports self-study and develops entrepreneurial thinking in the context of the cultural circumstances of Slovakia's regions, strengthening cultural literacy, creativity and inventiveness.

Trends in education policy at international level have led to the promotion of cultural knowledge, creativity and intercultural understanding through cultural education, within which the key elements of culture, art and cultural heritage are implemented in both general and technical education.

Based on the belief that education should respect the needs of a constantly changing multicultural society and reflect societal issues, we apply in research activities and teaching practice an approach using the development of cultural competencies in the context of the use of cultural heritage in upper secondary education with a focus on tourism.

The technical subjects, concerning the profile of graduates from the fields of study with a focus on tourism, are indispensable and important components in shaping their personalities. Implementation of elements of cultural heritage, in the development of professional competencies, expands their knowledge and experience. It is also a prerequisite for their successful entry into working life and, moreover, we cannot forget the fact that this will increase the ability of students to present Slovakia as a tourist destination.

Aspects of implementing cultural heritage in the educational process are significant not only in terms of the transfer of knowledge, facts and information about cultural heritage and in terms of cultivation and improvement of the individual, but they have direct scope in the formation of a culturally competent generation recognizing their cultural identity: a generation that has a demand for culture and cultural activities and is ready to live life in a multicultural society.

In the educational process, it is necessary to create or respectively shape the tools that can awaken awareness of cultural needs in students. Cultural education should greatly contribute to the growth of interest in culture in Slovak society. Acquisition and improvement of cultural competence as one of the core competencies should be developed in school education by moving toward educational objectives worthy of a civilized society and it should form the basis for lifelong learning.

Dominika Drábová

A contribution on the historical demography of Kysuce based on the example of the village of Oščadnica

Abstract: The chapter describes the population analysis in the catholic parish of Oščadnica in Kysuce region in the 19th century. The research was established especially on the analysis of church registers of births, marriages and burials. Researched majority population lived in depression of the creek Oščadnica and the rest of villagers occupied the surrounding solitudes (kopanice). The aim is to summarize the development of population growth, births, and deaths in Oščadnica in the19th century.

Keywords: History, demography, deaths, births, jobs, Oščadnica

Location and delimitation of territory[1]

The villag e of Oščadnica is located in the south of the Kysuce region in the Čadca district near the border with Poland and the Czech Republic. Oščadnica neighbors the villages of Skalité, Svrčinovec, Čierne, Zborov nad Bystricou, Klubina and the towns of Čadca and Krásno nad Kysucou. The village forms a typical chainlike pattern and along with its remote settlements is 14 kilometers long.[2]

Population is concentrated along the stream in the Oščadničanka valley and in the former remote settlements and mountain hamlets of Kubuši, Zagrapa, Michajkovia, Rovné, Beskydok, Svancari, Košariská, Peniaci, Vreščovka, Furmanec, Hanzlov, Magura, Čertež, Kubánkovia, Zvonári, Komanovky, Gošíci, Zadedová, Haladeji, Lalíci, Prední a Zadní Moskali, Vojtúšiza Dedovou and Košariská pod Račou.[3]

The stream has tributaries on both sides, the largest of them are, on the left, the Hanzlov, the Dirgasov, the Hrabovec (from Rovne), and in

---

1   Basic map of district Čadca 1: 50 000.
2   Memorial Book of village Oščadnica, 19.
3   Memorial Book of village Oščadnica, 22–23.

the southern part of the village, the Kučákov brooks. From the right side, under the cemetery, the Dedovka flows into the Oščadničanka stream. The Oščadničanka empties into the Kysuca river, near the manor house in the southern part of the village.

The valley is surrounded by relatively high mountains; from the south these are Kalinov hill (816 meters), Dedová (917 meters) and Veľká Rača, the highest Kysuce peak (1,236 meters). From the north there is Javorské hill (860 meters) and Liesková hill (850 meters), and from the east Vreščovský Beskyd (820 meters), Kykuľa (1,087 meters), Malý Príslop (985 meters) and Veľký Príslop (1,044 meters).

Property conditions and settlement of Oščadnica

The origins of the village of Oščadnica as well as numerous other villages in the upper Kysuce region are connected with the colonization by the Vlachs. The process of settlement was influenced by the struggle for power in the territory conducted by two manors, Budatín and Strečno. They both tried to impose themselves in this former frontier land, which gained attraction after the arrival of the Vlachs. Locations in the Oščadnica area such as Blasovicz and Diedova are mentioned as early as 1536. Attempts to found a village had occurred in the 1580s, but they were not successful, because the lords of these manors demolished each other's houses and property, stole livestock and even killed each other. The situation had to be solved by trial. According to the verdict, the territory of contemporary Oščadnica was divided between both manors, Budatín and Strečno. Both of them established their own village. The village of the Budatín manor was called Podjavorské, and it is first mentioned in 1613. The village of the Strečno manor bearing the name Oščadnica was first referred to as a village in 1624.[4] Ultimately, Strečno asserted its rights and won the conflict. The dispute was definitively concluded in 1769, when Mikuláš

---

4   Until the present day the question of the founding of the village of Oščadnica has not been satisfactorily answered. It is not clear if there were two villages – Oščadnica and Podjavorské – or there was just one, which was referred to by the Strečno and Budatín manors by different names. The final name of Oščadnica is apparently connected with Strečno's victory in the dispute with Budatín. Velička, *Osídlenie Kysúc*, 168–169.

Esterházy, landlord of the Strečno manor, purchased several Kysuce villages, including Oščadnica, from John Nepomuk Suňog.[5]

The Vlachs who were used by the Budatín and Strečno landlords to populate their territories were probably not originally ethnic Vlachs. Some of them were people from these manors, who were allowed by their landlords to change over to the Vlach way of life. Some of the new inhabitants may, according to Marsina, have come from Orava.[6] Other settlers emerged from northern Moravia especially from the locality of Tešín, which "…is reflected in the organization of mountain farming and sheep farm buildings from around Čadca, mainly in Oščadnica."[7]It is important to say that the flood of settlers was not only unidirectional but bidirectional. Parish registers testify to this fact with marriage records between lords from both sides of the frontier. There were a significant number of Polish newcomers. According to a report from 1673 around 2,500 people emigrated from the Žywiec manor to Slovakia.[8] Toponyms such as *U Poľky*, *Poluvka* and *U Poľačka* provide testimony of Polish origins. Likewise we know toponyms such as *Moravska* or *Moravske* indicate roots from Moravia.

Vlach colonization continued in the secluded mountain hamlets – known as "kopaničiar" hamlets – in the 16th and 17th centuries. Landlords forced the Vlachs to settle. They put in charge particular settlers who oversaw the settling of Vlach newcomers with their families, as well as non-Vlach inhabitants. These chosen settlers ensured people fulfilled their duties – paying taxes and Vlach dues, providing labor and a new form of due, which was wood in various forms.[9] The chosen steward – "scultetus" in Latin – enjoyed privileges in comparison with other villagers. He was provided with a larger plot of land, milling rights, the right to have an alehouse and butchery rights. At the same time, he was also a reeve and this function and other rights he passed down hereditarily.[10] The steward

---

5   Paráčová, *Spory panstiev Strečno a Budatín o hranice na Kysuciach*, 33–34.
6   Marsina, *K starším dejinám Kýsúc*, 75.
7   Bednárik, *Ľudové staviteľstvo na Kysuciach*, 110.
8   Bednárik, *Ľudové staviteľstvo na Kysuciach*, 13.
9   Beňko, *Osídlenie Kýsúc*, 29.
10 Rebro, *Urbárska regulácia Márie Terézie a poddanské úpravy Jozefa II.na Slovensku*, 425.

family in Oščadnica was named Kucharčík until the Theresian urbarium, when the institution of hereditary reeves was abolished.[11]

The territory of the newly founded village of Oščadnica was divided into precise parts hides – zárubky.[12] A hide was a parallel strip of soil from one edge of an area to another. Each settler's family got the tenancy of one hide, which became the basis of the family's household. The land was free of taxes for 6–20 years. During this period the householders had to transform woodland by hewing and grubbing them into pastures, meadows and arable land, so they were able to fulfill their duties toward their landlords.[13] In Oščadnica, the center of the household dooryard – plac – was situated in the valley. It took the name of its founder. Borders between hides were defined by hidepaths. Every hide included a household, communal cattle-run, field, meadows, sheep hut or possible location for it, valley road and brook.[14] A hide was measured by "days". A unit of "one day" comprised the area of arable land that could be ploughed with cows in one day.[15] Oščadnica consisted of 40 hides[16] which made it one of the largest villages in comparison with other villages in the Kysuce region, which usually had a size of 6 to 27 hides.[17] Oščadnica became a typical mountain hamlet village, expanding along the Oščadničanka stream, whereby developed the chainlike pattern of the village at the bottom of the valley with remote settlements in the hills.[18]

---

11 Rebro, *Urbárska regulácia Márie Terézie a poddanské úpravy Jozefa II.na Slovensku*, 429.
12 The word zárubek, pl. Zárubky comes from the Slovak verb rúbať – to lumber. This system of dividing land between settlers is unique to Kysuce.
13 Paráčová, *Z histórie lesníctva na Kysuciach*, 34.
14 Bednárik, *Ľudové staviteľstvo na Kysuciach*, 28–29.
15 Bednárik, *Ľudové staviteľstvo na Kysuciach*, 20.
16 The zárubky were: Gaborov, Šulganov, Ševčikov, Knapikov, Revajov, Hluchovsky, Kvasnicov, Drachnov, Škripkov, Školov, Kučakov, Penyov, Fefkov, Špalkov, Mruščakov, Riboňov, Kubušov, Kaszprov, Vojtušov, Kozov, Mroškovsk, Gajdošov, Majov, Angyelov, Mosorovlower, Mosorovupper, Pazderov, Kopačkov, lower Jendrišakov, Kvašnov, upper Jendrišakov, Gaulov, Chlastakov, Margušov, Dirgasov, Blahov, Lušňakov, Kancerov, Vresťov and the steward's was Kucharčíkov.
17 Beňko, *Osídlenie Kysúc*, 29.
18 Bednárik, *Ľudové staviteľstvo na Kysuciach*, 24.

Employment of inhabitants

Agriculture

The daily subsistence of virtually all residents of the Kysuce region depended on agriculture, including those who had other employment. In church registers, all villagers were marked as "colons"[19] even if they, according to village documents, had another job such as bricklayer, carpenter etc. Also the parish priest and innkeeper had their own household.[20] The upland nature of Kysuce had an effect on the fertility and quality of arable soil. In spite of the poor quality of the soil, agriculture represented the most common livelihood until the second half of the 20th century. They cultivated narrow, rocky fields which perched along the contours of slopes and hills shaped into terraces, where the people of Oščadnica tried to make use of every piece of land. The largest of the stones alongside the fields are evident in terrain up to the present day. Another problem was also the thin layer of topsoil; its fertility was always minimal. The low yields from the fields were caused by ineffective fertilizing.[21] On the highest-located farms only oats of an inferior sort, small potatoes and cabbage were produced. In the valley, where the soil was a little more fertile they rarely grew rye and barley.

In the second half of the 17th century a type of estate called an allodium[22] was founded in Oščadnica. This estate existed until the second half of the 19th century. It was located at the edge of village in an area called "Pod Oščadnicou" in the surroundings of the present-day manor house.[23] According to the allodium plans from 1808, the estate consisted of two mills, a saw, a brewery, an inn, a toll station, manor buildings and houses for servants and officials, stables, sheepfolds, fields, pastures and a place for breeding snails.[24] Rye, barley, oats, flax, hemp and hemp seed were

---

19 Colonus – a type of farmer with inheritable rights to a piece of land, but who didn't own the land.
20 Parish records; accounts of the village Oščadnica, State archive in Bytča (SA BY); contract of leasing the inn at the manor, SA BY.
21 Memorial Book of the village of Oščadnica, 97–99.
22 Allodium – land freely held, without obligation of service to any overlord.
23 Memorial Book of the village of Oščadnica, 64.
24 Plan of the allodium in Oščadnica, SA BY.

cultivated there. At the beginning of the 19th century there was even an attempt to grow hops there. Beef-cattle, sheep and pigs were bred. Thick and thin linen, wool, butter, curd cheese and sheep cheese were produced.[25] In the brewery, beer was brewed until the turn of the 19th century.[26] The head of the estate was the "majer" or allodiary, who reported to the higher manor officials in the running of the estate.[27] The allodiaries were from the Gabor family; in 1802 the position of majer was held by Juraj Gábor. He took care of 60 cows, oxen, bulls and calves. To carry out this work, he hired servants and then oversaw their care of the livestock.[28] He also managed work conducted by villagers who were assigned duties by the Theresian urbarium.[29]

Lumbering, processing and the lumber trade

People tried to find supplementary jobs if possible, in addition to agriculture. One option in Kysuce was to work in the forests. Wood was burned into charcoal, or when the stream overflowed, raftsmen floated the logs down the stream into the Kysuca River and then further on to southern parts of Hungary.[30] Wood in many forms was part of Kysuce's specific mountain hamlet produce – inhabitants sent their feudal landlords logs, boards and wooden shingle.

The sawmill at the manor was first mentioned in the urbarium in 1658. Inhabitants of Oščadnica and neighboring villages went there to work.[31] The oldest known tenant of the sawmill was miller Juraj Plaček, who leased the saw for 15-and-a-half golden coins per year in 1781.[32] After him the saw was in 1784 leased by Ignác Lipták for 20 golden coins per year for three years. In 1789, Lipták and Plaček leased the saw together for 35

25 Zatloukalová, *Poddanské dediny mesta Žiliny (Závodie, Krásno nad Kysucou, Horelica, Oščadnica, Zborov)*, 158.
26 Drábová, *Majer v Oščadnici v období rokov 1770–1850*, 75–84.
27 Paráčová, *Panstvo Strečno (náčrt vzniku, vývoja a majetkových vzťahov)*, 45.
28 Contracts, SA BY.
29 Theresian urbarium documents of the village of Oščadnica, SA BY.
30 Memorial Book of the village of Oščadnica, 113–114.
31 Urbarium of the village Oščadnica from 1658.
32 Income sheet and register of villages of the Strečno manor, SA BY.

golden coins yearly.[33] Their duty was to work at the sawmill for the manor and saw as many logs as it needed. The saw was indeed profitable and rent rose over the years. In 1813, the saw along with the mill were rented by Jozef Trúchly and innkeeper Marek Spitzer for 150 golden coins per year. Later in 1820, Ján Kubica and his wife leased the saw. After them their son Štefan Kubica, who was mentioned in a contract from 1846, continued the work. An inventory from 1849 was signed by Matej Kubica. It is possible to observe a change in the leasing system here. The saw-millers did not pay any rent but instead received a yearly salary. In return they were obliged to saw the manor's logs. If they ran out of logs, they were allowed to saw someone else's logs, but for that they had to pay a tax into the landlord's coffers. Tenants were obliged to maintain all equipment belonging to the sawmill. In case of any damage to the property, they were obliged to recompense it. Kubica's function was to manage the work at the saw. The manor provided repairs and the supply of wood.[34]

A second watermill was leased by a Jewish inhabitant of nearby Čadca, Jakub Neuwirth, for six years from January 1, 1791 for 50 golden coins yearly. Under the penalty of 12 golden coins, he had to avoid buying stolen wood. A quarter of a year before the contract came to an end he was to announce whether he was willing to prolong the contract, or the manor would have to look for a new tenant. There is no more information known on this water saw. In the past it was common to merge saw- and watermills. It is possible that this water-powered saw belonged to one of six mills and therefore was no longer mentioned separately in the sources.[35]

Mayor Juraj Trúchly was a businessman who dealt in lumber. Wood was at first lumbered in the forest and then sold in Kysucké Nové Mesto and Žilina.[36] For example, in 1838, he prepared lumber products consisting of 800 boards and 3,000 laths to the value of 498 golden coins on the river bank and waited for the water to be high enough so that he could send the goods down-river by hired raftsmen.[37] Trúchly sold 15 raft-loads worth

33 Contracts, SA BY.
34 Contracts, SA BY.
35 Contracts, SA BY.
36 Criminal and civil cases of the villages of the Strečno manor. SA BY.
37 Criminal and civil cases of the villages of the Strečno manor. SA BY.

203 golden and 12 silver coins to citizens of Žilina. However Trúchly let this lumber material wait on the river bank for a long time and it partly decreased in value because of that, after which he sold the same products to another buyer. Therefore the citizens of Žilina took him to court. There were also other penalties waiting for him there, other discontent customers and finally debts for alcohol purchased from the innkeeper's widow, Spitzer.[38]

In 1862, the large-scale entrepreneur and lumber baron Leopold Popper leased the former Strečno manor from the Esterházy family. He set up a lumber warehouse in Oščadnica. After his death in 1886, his son Armín Popper inherited the property and sold it on. In 1916, a steam-powered sawmill was founded here.[39]

Craft industries

As mentioned previously, many people took second jobs alongside farming their fields or worked as seasonal journey workers, who annually left their homes so they could earn extra money in southern parts of Hungary. In 1781, five weavers and one blacksmith operated in the village.[40] Weavers here were called "knop" from which is derived the dwelling name "U knapika". Although the sources do not mention them, they were common even in the 20th century.[41] In 1786, Ignác Lipták requested that the manor grant him permission to build a fulling mill on the Oščadnica stream. He won approval and had to pay five golden coins per year,[42] but there is no further evidence of the fulling mill later, so it can be assumed that it is closed. In the Majak family, there were carpenters who repaired the foundations of the clergy house in 1813, after flooding had damaged them.[43] Another instance of a carpenter was Matej Špaček, who worked on a new clergy house in 1843.[44]

---

38 Criminal and civil cases of the villages of the Strečno manor. SA BY.
39 Parish chronicle, 32.
40 Documentum communitatum 1781, SA BY.
41 Memorial Book of the village of Oščadnica, 105–107.
42 Contracts, SA BY.
43 Visitation of the parish of Oščadnica from 1828.
44 Accounts of the village of Oščadnica, SA BY.

There were six farmer's mills and one manor mill in Oščadnica. Farmer's mills were mentioned in the regular earnings of the Strečno manor. In the first records, six mills were regularly mentioned: four farmer's mills, one steward's mill and one paper mill. In 1819, the following millers were mentioned: Vojtuš, Smolka, Piniak, Kučák, the steward and Šulgan with his paper mill.[45] Four identical contracts were drawn up with each of the farm millers in 1831. The first belonged to Ján Vojtuš and Michal Blahovec; the second to Ján Piniak and Matúš Vrábel; the third was operated by Jozef, Ondrej, Ján and Michal Smolka; the fourth mill was operated by Ján and Jakub Kučák together with Ján and Ondrej Škola. This mill was located on the left side of the stream, near the bridge and the present-day bus stop "U Vojtuša".[46] The fifth mill, the steward's mill, belonged to the Kucharčík family.[47] The paper mill had already existed before 1770; it was drawn on the first military survey maps. In the Strečno manor books, Ján Šulgan was recorded as a miller, who paid eight golden coins per year for the right to operate his mill.[48] After him sources refer to his descendant Jozef Šulgan, who worked there in 1831 and rented the mill for 18 golden coins.[49] The mill ceased to exist in the second half of the 19th century. It was situated on the left side of the stream in the household "U Drába". The toponym "Zapaperňu" is used here to the present day.[50]

Ethnic and national composition

The northern regions of the Hungarian Kingdom were traditionally populated by Slovak inhabitants. Oščadnica was ethnically a Slovak village. Gypsies, who according to parish registers lived here at the end of the 19th century, were an exception. An example was the family of the blacksmith, Baláž. Other ethnic groups included the recently arrived Jews – they

---

45 Income sheet and register of the villages of the Strečno manor, SA BY.
46 Source, Jozef Dráb.
47 Income sheet and register of the villages of the Strečno manor, SA BY.
48 Accounts of the Strečno manor, SA BY.
49 Contracts, SA BY.
50 Parish chronicle, 21; Memorial Book of the village of Oščadnica, 62; the paper mill was located in the present-day (2017) gardens of Plevko, Deman and Kučak. Source, Jozef Dráb.

came from German-speaking areas or from Czech and Polish territories.
A similar situation occurred with manor officials, clerks and tradesmen.
In the second half of the 19th century, there were more people claiming
to be Hungarian, in an ethnic not geographical sense, and they were also
arriving in Kysuce along with the modernization and bureaucratization of
society.

Religious affiliation

One of the attributes of Kysuce cultural identity is religious affiliation.
A close relationship with Christianity "from womb to tomb" formed generations of Kysuce inhabitants for centuries. Deep faith was an essential
part of everyday life. The way of life, customs, habits and folk literature
were connected with Christianity.

The majority of villages, Oščadnica included, were founded by
Protestant feudal lords. Following "Quius regio, eius religio", the denom-
ination of dwellers was Protestant as well.[51] The subsequent Catholic
tradition of Kysuce is a result of consistent recatholicization, which was
promoted in several ways. Feudal lords converted first and then their serfs
too. Some weight must be assigned to the Franciscan brothers from Žilina.
Recatholicization was finally completed by the establishment of the new
so-called Josephinian parishes, almost in every larger village. In Oščadnica,
a parish was established in August 1789.[52] At the end of the 18th century,
the Kysuce region was largely a homogenous Catholic territory with the
exception of the recently arrived Jewish community.

Roman Catholics – parish history

Oščadnica has always been a large village. There was a great need for its
own parish; however for a long time it administratively came under the
parish in Čadca and later, in 1749, it became a branch of the parish of
Skalité. In 1767, in Oščadnica there was just a cemetery and bell tower.[53]

---

51 Paráčová, *Evanjelicke Kysuce a rekatolizacia*, 37–50.
52 Velička, *Otazka zalozenia katolickych farnosti na hornych Kysuciach v 17.
   a v I. polovici 18. Storocia*, 59–78.
53 Velička, *Zaniknuté drevené kostoly v kysuckom Pobeskydí II.*, 13.

Villagers made a serious effort to build a new church. In observations added to the First Military Survey from 1769, it is mentioned that a proper church would be erected in the village.[54] Also in the Strečno manor administrator's documents from 1772, it was written that villagers had already prepared the material to build the church and they would devote it to St. Anna.[55] Despite this, the church was only finished in 1787. The parish was established one year later as one of the Josephinian parishes. The church was consecrated in 1788 by Lukáš Pažický and dedicated to St. Stephen the King of Hungary.[56] The first priest was Kuba Damasus, Franciscan and member of The Slovak Scholarly Society, as was his successor Ján Škorvánek.[57] In the period from 1788–1918, 14 priests and 16 chaplains were in charge of the parish.[58]

The wooden church was merely provisional. It served believers only for 16 years, and in 1804 a new brick church was built.[59] The church was not consecrated but only blessed by Deputy Archdeacon Juraj Gézy in 1807. In 1828, the curator of the church was Jozef Trúchly. It seems that he inherited the function from his father.[60]

Reverence for the Virgin Mary is a part of Oščadnica people's identity. A statue placed on a tetragonal stone column called a "trinity" – *trojička*– was placed in a tree hollow just off the road in Kozovzárubek in 1830. The

---

54 *EingrosseszestreütesDorfliegt im PiniowkaThalwirdeinesolideKircherbaut im Dorf…* Azelsőkatonaifelméres. DVD Arcanum, Budapest, 2002.
55 Velička, *Zaniknuté drevené kostoly v kysuckom Pobeskydí II.*, 13.
56 In the 18th and 19th centuries, there was a magyar national revival, demonstrated also in the renaissance of Hungarian patron saints. It sometimes happened that they replaced existing patron saints as well, so when they replaced Anna with King St. Stephen it wasn't so unusual. Podoláková, *Patronícia kysuckých chrámov a významné sakrálne pamiatky Kysúc*, 106.
57 The Slovak Scholary Society was an association of Bernolák collaborators and sympathizers, which united mainly priests. They propagated the Slovak language, wrote books and distributed them to the common people. Oščadnica together with other Kysuce villages belonged under the branch of The Slovak Scholary Society in Veľké Rovné. Belás, *Pôsobenie kysuckých kňazov v pobočnom stánku Slovenského učeného tovaryšstva vo Veľkom Rovom – Kysuckí kňazi bernolákovci*, 99–101.
58 Parish chronicle, 29.
59 Parish chronicle, 1 and 9.
60 Visitation of the parish of Oščadnica from 1828.

statue represented the coronation of the Virgin Mary by the Holy Trinity. It was later stolen and the shrine was recreated in 1940.[61]

The clergy house was built in 1788 near the original church. It had two rooms for a priest and family. In 1813, an unexpected flood destroyed the clergy house foundations. They were repaired by serfs from the Majak family for four golden coins from the village municipality. In 1819, two stables and two wine cellars covered with a reed roof were added to the clergy house.[62] The clergy house was still inhabited in 1828, although its condition must not have been optimal, because a new clergy house was built in 1838–1843.[63] This was a four-room house with windows oriented toward the church, of which three rooms served as priests' quarters and the fourth was used by the chaplain and had a separate entrance.[64]

School

The Roman Catholic folk school was first mentioned in the visitation of the parish in 1798.[65] The wooden school building had one room and two separate entrances. It did not have its own garden. Children were taught in Slovak. The first teacher was Mikuláš Lovišek. He was an honorable man, had good command of Latin and was especially capable of teaching the young.[66] The building served its purpose until 1825. After that the villagers built a new wooden school with two rooms. The school had a garden as well; it neighbored upon the parish garden. Jozef Kastulay from Čierne was the teacher and organist. He was married and therefore provided a bedroom with two beds, so that he was able to devote himself to profane affairs as well as sacred ones.[67]

Literacy was virtually non-existent; however in the middle of the 19th century, it increased as a result of the activities of the church school. More

---

61 Parish chronicle, 24.
62 Parish chronicle, 9.
63 Accounts of the village of Oščadnica, SA BY.
64 Parish chronicle, 9.
65 Visitation of the parish Oščadnica from 1798.
66 Parish chronicle, 16; Kralovičová, *Prehľad katolíckeho školstva na Kysuciach do I. pol. 20. Storočia*, 174.
67 Parish chronicle, 16.

frequent signatures on official documents appeared and a decrease in three x-s instead of a signature. It is probable that people could not write, but the ability to read was more widespread.

Jewish community

The Jewish community started to form in the Kysuce region during the course of the 18th century, although in a few isolated cases there are some references to Jewish inhabitants also from earlier periods. Their arrival was a reaction to the Edict of Tolerance of 1782 issued by Emperor Joseph II. They arrived in the Kingdom of Hungary and to the Kysuce region from the Czech regions of Moravia and Silesia because of more advantageous legal conditions, but they were not given equal status to the domestic population. One of these restraints was the prohibition of buying land, which therefore caused problems with the building or purchasing of a house. The Kysuce region was not a very attractive destination so they stopped there just for a short stay. The main disadvantages of the Kysuce region were poverty and backwardness followed by low opportunity of earning for both merchants and craftsmen. Consequently, the number of Jews was lower in this region compared to southern neighboring regions.[68] In spite of this situation, the number of Jews grew little by little each year. Many of them opened their own stores or sold wares in taverns. Besides this they worked as craftsmen, officials and wood merchants, but some of them were poor and religion was the only thing that distinguished them from the majority population.[69] Jews acted as the renters of manor amenities such as taverns, sawmills, slaughterhouses and breweries.

David Rozenfeld was among the first Jews in Oščadnica. He leased the inn near the church and slaughterhouse. He left the village after three years. In 1794, Marek Spitzer leased the inn and in 1797 a Jew from Čadca, Jozef Joachim, rented the saw.[70] Another innkeeper was Marek Samuel, who worked in the brewery in 1803.[71] According to the Jewish register of the

---

68 Hudecová, *Formovanie židovskej komunity na Kysuciach do konca 18. Storočia*, 59–73.
69 Liščák, *Čadca v prvej polovici 19.storočia*, 72.
70 Contracts, SA BY.
71 Criminal and civil cases of the villages of Strečno manor. SA BY.

Strečno manor from the 1820s, there were no Jews living in Oščadnica until 1828.[72] Ľudovít Nagy asserted the same information in his population encyclopedia from 1828.[73] However, inns were rented by Marek Spitzer, who lived in Raková and had come to Kysuce from Moravia. Jozef Frankl, 34 at the time, came to Oščadnica in August 1828 from the neighboring village of Stará Bystrica. Frankl and Samuel Spitzer, who came to Oščadnica one year later, were both innkeepers. According to Strečno manor records, Samuel was 28 and lived in his inn nearby the church.[74] In 1844, three Spitzer brothers and their families lived there. Marek had an inn by the manor, Lazar with his wife Tereza by the church and the third brother, Adolf, built a new inn halfway between two old ones.[75]

Oščadnica's chronicles inform us about four families in 1857. Alojz Spitzer had an inn, store and later also the sawmill near the church. His youngest brother Marek had an inn by the manor house on the crossroads. The middle inn belonged to Jabub Spitzer. It is very interesting that the three Spitzer brothers owned three inns, as in 1844. The difference is in their names, which may have been just adjusted to the Slovak language. The fourth Jew was Herman Pausinger, with his family. He had the inn in the upper part of the village. He made several journeys to America together with some Oščadnica inhabitants. Descendants of these families still lived in Oščadnica in the 20th century.[76]

Population development

Population development is a result of natural (natality and mortality) and mechanical phenomena (migration). It is influenced by war, lack of food, disease, migration, social issues and the economy.[77]

According to the parish visitation protocol in 1788, Oščadnica had 2,359 inhabitants.[78] The register of dwellings mentions 329 houses in

---

72 Register of Jews in Strečno manor.
73 Nagy, *Notitiaepolitico-geographico-statisticae inclyti regni Hungariae partiumqueeidemadnexarum*, 411.
74 Income sheet and register of the villages of Strečno manor, SA BY.
75 Income sheet and register of the villages of Strečno manor, SA BY.
76 Memorial Book of the village of Oščadnica, 257.
77 Lauko and Tolmáči, *Humánna geografia Slovenskej republiky*, 4.
78 Velička, *Zaniknuté drevené kostoly v kysuckom Pobeskydí II.*, 13.

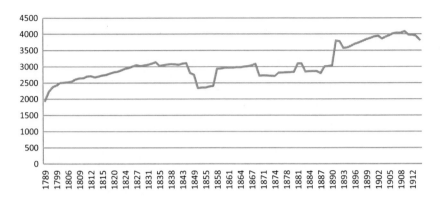

Tab. 1: Population development in Oščadnica in 1789–1922

1795.[79] The population grew (Tab. 1.), but on the contrary the number of houses did not. The Second Military Survey Map (1806–1811) recorded 271 houses.[80] Population growth slowed down in the 1820s. Nagy writes about 306 houses and 2978 inhabitants, nine inhabitants per house on average.[81] In 1836, there were 405 houses[82] in Oščadnica and in 1847, 438 houses in 39 settlements, in which lived 350 families and 49 lodgers[83] (dispersed settlements not included). Some inhabitants owned more than just one house, for instance, Ondrej Drahošan from Gaulov's settlement had six houses.[84] The most significant population crisis occurred at the end of the 1840s; in Kysuce this crisis is known as "the years of decline". Kysuce were affected by what was historically its largest typhus epidemic combined with famine. The reaction was a collective emigration to southern parts of the monarchy, which was in the 1870s replaced by emigration to

---

79 Register of settlements of the village of Oščadnica in 1795, 1836. SA BY.

80 Austrian State Archive/MilitaryArchive, Vienna (ÓsterreichichesStaatsarchiv), Second Military Survey section No. 31–32, 31–33.

81 Nagy, *Notitiaepolitico-geographico-statisticae inclyti regni Hungariae partiumqueeidemadnexarum*, 411.

82 Register of settlement of the village of Oščadnica in 1795, 1836. SA BY.

83 A subinquilinus was a person without any property, who lived with another family in their house for work and food.

84 Income sheet and register of villages of the Strečno manor, SA BY.

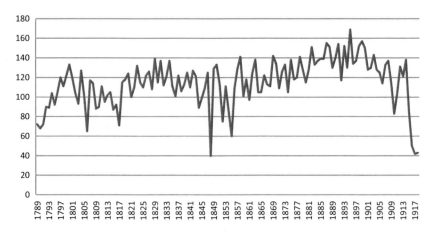

Tab. 2: Natality in Oščadnica in 1789–1918

America. In spite of the great number of emigrants, the population started to rise slightly and this continued until the First World War (Tab. 1).

Natality

Natality is the ratio between the number of live births in an area and the population of that area. It is expressed by the number of births per 1000 of population per year.[85] Natality in Oščadnica had a variable curve (Tab. 2). From 1790 to 1819, the average birth rate was 68. In the next two decades, it grew to 108 and it held around that average until the 1870s. In the last decades of the 19th century, natality rose to 130 on average. At the beginning of the 20th century, it decreased slightly. During the First World War, natality was just 40 per year.[86] The majority of children were legitimate; however sometimes illegitimate children were born, on average one per year. These children used to be given uncommon names. It was a form of punishment for premarital sex. The instigators were not parents but usually priests, who baptized the child with that kind of name. Children of unknown fathers were rare; they used to be given the name Ignatius, but

---

85 Available on internet: http://www.thefreedictionary.com/natality.
86 Parish records.

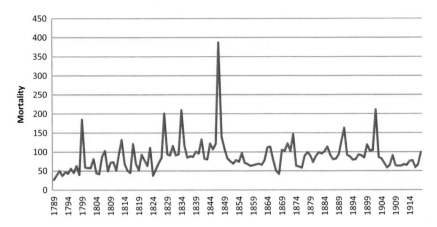

Tab. 3: Mortality in Oščadnica in 1789–1922

later the custom was abandoned. Twins were sometimes born, usually at a rate of one pair per year. If they were a boy and girl, they received the names Adam and Eva. One of them was usually named Adam even when they were two boys. In cases of two girls, Eva was not so frequent. In 1793, triplets were born, but one boy died soon after birth.[87]

Mortality

Mortality is the relative frequency of deaths in a specific population, also known as the death rate.[88] The average mortality held at around 80 per year, but in the 19th century, epidemics and natural disasters were not rare (Tab. 3). I focused on the years 1813, 1817, 1831 and 1846–1848. These events resonated greatly during the periods when they took place, as they do today. There were other epidemics of cholera in the 1860s and a major one in 1873, but they did not impact on the collective memory as the years of decline in the 1840s or the cholera outbreak in 1831.

1813 was the year of the great flood; contemporaries declared it a one-in-a-thousand-year deluge.[89] A great wave destroyed the foundations of

---

87 Parish records.
88 Available on internet: http://www.thefreedictionary.com/mortality.
89 Laš, *Skalité, obec pod Trojačkom*, 155.

the clergy house. Mortality in this year increased, but it was not due to the flood. According to parish records, children mostly died at the beginning of the year. Another disaster came in 1816 as a result of the Tambour volcano eruption on April 10, 1815. It ejected large amounts of ash and aerosols into the stratosphere; it had an effect on the climate. 1816 is well known as a year without a summer and without crops.[90] It was naturally followed by famine and great loss of life. This fully manifested itself in the following year of 1817. In Oščadnica, 121 people of 2,732 died, which amounted to 4 % of the population.[91] In subsequent years, mortality was around the average until 1828. Church records did not note the cause of deaths of 201 inhabitants, but information from a neighboring village about typhus could explain the increased death rate.[92] The major mortality in 1828 meant that cholera in 1831 did not have as fatal consequences as in other villages; Oščadnica experienced only 116 deaths in that year, thus deaths by cholera may have been around 30 in comparison to Čadca, where 158 people died in the month of September alone,[93] or in Stará Bystrica with 82 deaths, where they needed to establish new cemeteries.[94] People tried to cure cholera with juniper oil, vinegar and some unknown spices.[95] A further blow for the villagers was the dry year 1834 with 210 dead, and 1835 with 117 dead. Even more fatal than previous plagues was a famine that appeared in 1846 culminating in 1847, and lasting until 1848. It preceded a bad crop in previous years. The parish chronicle recounts: *"In the previous year the crop was poor in the village. Import of food because of miserable roads and a total absence of railways was limited, and it resulted in famine and afterwards epidemic typhus. 242 adults succumbed to epidemic typhus in 1847. In 1848 epidemic typhus still endured but it did not have the great scale as the year before, when from 138 dead 69 had died of epidemic typhus."*[96] Altogether, in 1846, 121 people died; in

90 Liščák, *Čadca v prvej polovici 19.Storočia*, 46.
91 Parish records.
92 Holáč chronicle – transcription. SA Čadca (CA)
93 Liščák, *Z nových výskumov k dejinám Čadce v prvej polovici 19. Storočia*, 123–124.
94 Liščák, *Z nových výskumov k dejinám Čadce v prvej polovici 19.Storočia*, 61.
95 Liščák, *Deti Bystríc*, 62.
96 Parish chronicle, 36.

1847, 387 died and in 1848, 140 died.[97] People milled sawdust and tree bark and out of this they cooked pulp or baked pancakes; they ate grass, nettles and potato haulm.[98] The terrible situation was worsened by alcoholism. Many people used potatoes even in this time to distil alcohol.[99] The high level of mortality caused problems with the burial of corpses. A lot of surrounding villages established new graveyards, but often it was not enough. Because of this mass graves were excavated. In Oščadnica, there was one under the present-day road in front of the clerical house, called by locals "slaked lime" – with which this mass grave was filled and then covered by soil. Information about this grave was not written anywhere, but bridal processions avoided this place and used to take a longer path to the church, because it was believed that it could bring bad fortune. Today this information has largely been forgotten and is known only by people living nearby.

---

97 Parish records.
98 Memorial Book of the village of Oščadnica, 103.
99 Velička, *Dejiny farnosti Vysoká*, 89.

Martina Hrabovská

The development of the choreographic production of folklore ensembles in the Slovak folklore movement from the point of view of period dance esthetics in the second half of the 20th century

Abstract: Since the late 1940s, when we can talk about the beginning of the most striking wave of scenic folklorism in Slovakia, there have been many indirect testimonies in the literature about how folk dance choreography has evolved. However, the criticism that the choreographic work is facing today does not appear for the first time in the history of the folklore movement. The first serious level of debates about the professional direction of the folklore movement rose in the 1970s and 1980s. Leading representatives of ethnology, ethnochoreology, choreography and personalities of the folklore movement in Slovakia have noticed the need to guide the work of folk ensembles. This chapter aims to contribute to the debate by a retrospective view of choreographic work in the second half of the 20th century and its overlaps into the choreographic work of the present generation of creators.

Keywords: Choreographic work, stage folk dance, folklore movement

Stage folklorism in Slovakia has been the most popula r form in the representation of traditional folk culture for more than half a century. Amateur folklore ensembles, through choreographies of folk dance, are the main exponents of dance and music folklore (and other types of folk art) specific to a locality or region of Slovakia. Various forms of the representation of traditional folk culture on stage, via which the choreographic work in folklore ensembles in the history of the folklore movement[1] has usually been performed, have influenced the opinions and tastes of consumers of

---

1   The term folklore movement is used to characterize activities of folk ensembles, encompassing festivals, performances, competitions of staged forms of folk music and dance.

this type of art considerably. It is on the basis of these choreographies of folk dance that the ensembles create an impression of the traditional folk culture of Slovakia.

This depiction of folk culture – the "second" form, as we say in Folkloristics – whose first manifestations came at the end of the 19th century, have been exposed to contemporary esthetic criteria in each development period.

In this chapter, I will present the issue of the development of the folklore movement through the prism of the esthetic criteria of the folklore dance stage from the end of the 19th century, with the main focus on the second half of the 20th century. The defined period is delimited by two significant milestones. The first is in 1948, when the origin of the Slovak artistic ensemble *Lúčnica* officially defines the creation of an organized wave of stage presentation of traditional folk culture. I define the upper limit in 1992, when the publishing of Rytmus magazine,[2] which was one of the key sources of data for this study, ended. In addition to Rytmus magazine, an important source of information is interviews with selected choreographers[3] of folk dance, whose active choreographic activity falls within the study of the defined period.

This compilation of contemporary insights into the art production of amateur and professional folklore ensembles in Slovakia in the second half of the 20th century represents the first attempt to summarize the knowledge of contemporary dance esthetics and thus provides a reflective bridge for comparative study of this issue to the present.

---

2   Rytmus magazine, published from the 1960s to the 1990s, was a forum where experts reflected on the performance of amateur art in Slovakia. Population-educational contributions from the area of the folklore movement in Slovakia are today an important source of information and its individual developmental phases from the perspective of contemporaries.

3   On the basis of the pre-research for this thesis and the fact that I have been active in the folklore movement in Slovakia since 2012, I have divided choreographers working in the folklore movement in Slovakia into four generational groups, based on age and most active period of their choreographic production, which will serve to reflect changes in approach to the choreographic creation of folk dance in Slovakia.

The pre-history of the folklore movement: Forms of folk dance staging in Slovakia before World War II

The beginnings of the Hungarian nobility's interest in Slovak folk dance go back to the 16th and 17th centuries when able performers of herdsman's dances presented their art form in the nobles' courtyards – outside of their rural (natural) environment. In the 18th century, the first performances of folk customs and traditions in the context of coronation celebrations had already appeared. In connection with the abolition of 170 years of Latin school performances and their substitution for those in the mother tongue, well understood especially in student theatres, the folk song gained popularity, arriving in noble courts and also affecting the peace in places of worship.[4]

During this period, it is possible to talk about the historical roots of the first folk groups.[5] M. Slivka connects[6] their pre-history with the aforementioned opportunities afforded by presentation of folklore on the artistic stage, especially at the noble courts.[7]

The Enlightenment brought a new perspective on the many layers of folk. In connection with the teachings of the German philosopher Johann Gottfried von Herder, which had spread among the then Slovak

---

4 Švehlák, *Folklór a umenie dneška (k štúdiu folklorizmu v súčasnej kultúre)*, 24.
5 During the second half of the 20th century, two types of group dominated the folklore movement in Slovakia. The village folklore group represents the phenomena of local folk culture. The folklore group has a membership base that transcends age – from children to retired people. The choreography of the folklore group often uses the lowest degree of stylization, with the emphasis on demonstrating authentic forms of folk music and dance. In contrast, the folklore ensemble operates in the city. Its members are mostly people aged from 15 to 35 years. The repertoire is mostly tied to the region in which the ensemble resides. The choreography of the folklore ensemble can also be created with a higher degree of stylization.
6 Prof. PhDr. Martin Slivka, CSc. (1929–2002) was a film director, ethnographer and university lecturer. His most significant ethnographic films include the 13-part series *Folk Art in Slovakia* (1970–1975); films on folk masquerade theatre (1986); *Carnival* (1969); *The Carollers are Coming* (1986) and the 13-part series on the Roma people *Children of the Wind* (1989–1991) (Benža, 1995, p. 152–153).
7 Slivka, *K dejinám scénických foriem folkóru*, 11.

intelligentsia, educators sought to build the foundations of a moral society in the culture of rural people. They educated them and recognized its manifestations.[8]

These efforts culminated in the Romantic period (in Slovakia from the late 18th to the middle of the 19th century), when people began to collect, write and edit folk songs, highlighting their artistic value. The cultural life of the Slovak intelligentsia was entwined with the national spirit. The national revival contributed to the emergence of Slovak stagecraft, in which popular elements of folk culture were used and presented. The development of the folklore movement in Slovakia was affected in the 19th century by the institutions of the Slovak Matica[9] and the Slovak Museum Society,[10] but also by many associations that at that time fulfilled a role in raising the educational and national consciousness. A great interest at that time was reflected in folk art traditions, especially embroidery.[11]

At the end of the 19th and the beginning of the 20th century, the formation of the first folk groups (most often under the name of ethnographic group) is recorded, but they functioned in an unorganized way and only occasionally, especially with a view to one-off performances especially in the High Tatras, spa towns and other similar events.[12]

In 1895, a *Czechoslavic Ethnographic Exhibition* was held in Prague, which is generally known as the first organized public performance of Slovak folklore groups. There were folk groups from the Slovak villages of Čičmany, Detva, Vydrná and Maríková (Slivka, 1976, p. 11) that demonstrated the richness of the spiritual folk culture in Slovakia, Moravia and Bohemia through their performances in Prague. They performed their

---

8 Švehlák, *Folklór a umenie dneška (k štúdiu folklorizmu v súčasnej kultúre)*, 24.
9 Matica Slovenská (Slovak Matica) is a scientific and cultural institution focusing on national themes and was established in 1863 as a result of Slovak nationalist efforts to lay the foundations of Slovak science, libraries and museums.
10 The Slovak Museum Society (Slovenská muzeálna spoločnosť) was a scientific society established in 1893 in the town of Martin. It brought together those interested in gathering, looking after and making available the monuments and artifacts that represented the spiritual culture of the Slovaks. The main goals of the institute were the establishment of a national museum, libraries and the organization of homeland research and museological activities.
11 Zálešák, *Folklórne hnutie na Slovensku*, 8–10.
12 Zálešák, *Folklórne hnutie na Slovensku*, 10–11.

dances and songs in authentic costumes as stand-alone performances or as part of wedding ceremonies.

A change took place after the end of World War I and the establishment of the First Czechoslovak Republic in 1918. The revival of the *Slovak Matica* in 1919 was also a major part of this change. Various cultural events were organized where folklore played an important role in manifesting the joy of having acquired freedom and the emergence of the First Czechoslovak Republic: "The inter-war period was an important chapter in the history of the 'staged' forms of folklore, which were, during this period, a presentation of authentic forms on the stage".[13]

Among the most important cultural events of the onstage representation of authentic folklore organized at that time were the *National Festivities* held in various towns in Slovakia (Martin, Košice, Banská Bystrica, the spa towns) from 1926. They had a rich official and cultural program. Ethnographic groups from Važec, Nižný Hrabovec, Ždiar, Myslava, Vyšné Raslavice, Čičmany, Detva, Polomka, Zliechov were represented via them. The main organizer of the National Festivities was Matica Slovenská in cooperation with Prof. Karol Plicka[14] (Slivka, 1976, p. 11).

The period of World War II brought a general downturn in the cultural life of Slovakia. Folklore became a means of the manifestation of the power of the fascist representatives of the Slovak state, who used it to support its political goals (Zálešák, 1982, p. 11).

The situation changed after World War II. Slovakia, like other Central European countries, fell under the cultural influence of the Soviet Union. There was a rise of onstage forms of folklore representation, which gradually came under the patronage of organized and institutional support:

> The impetus for the creation of organized folklore ensembles was given by the Soviet song and dance ensembles (the Moiseyev Dance Company, the Alexandrov Ensemble and the Piatnicky Ensemble), who came to us immediately after the liberation. After their inimitable artistic performances, many became more aware of

---

13 Slivka, *K dejinám scénických foriem folklóru*, 11.

14 Igor Moiseyev was born in Kiev in 1906, but soon after his birth he moved to Paris with his parents. Dospievanie travelled to Russia with his father, during which he had the opportunity to learn the culture of different ethnic groups. Between 1924 and 1939, he was a member of the Bolshoi Theatre in Moscow, performing several times as a solo dancer.

the value of folk art, its progressiveness and its constant freshness. They started to think about establishing similar ensembles in our country.[15]

The staging of folk dance in the USSR

The previous quotation depicting the cultural and social situation in the post-war years of the folklore movement in Czechoslovakia illustrates the important role played by the Soviet ensembles and their specific way of staging folk dance (based on the dance traditions of the Russian romantic ballet) in the historical development of the production of folk dance in our country. In 1937, Igor Moiseyev founded the Moiseyev Dance Company, the first professional ensemble of its kind in the former USSR, which first staged folk dance as a separate dance genre – folklore ballet.[16]

In 1936, he was commissioned to organize a folk dance festival of all the republics of the USSR, whose selected dancers, in association with professional artists of the Bolshoi Theatre, formed the founding members of the Moiseyev Dance Company: "After several successful performances throughout the Soviet Union and Eastern Europe, all satellite countries began to set up folk ensembles imitating the Moiseyev model. 'Moiseyev's' ensembles could be seen across the entire Eastern Bloc".[17]

In its first years of existence, the ensemble was composed of professional dancers of the Bolshoi Theatre Ballet. Later on, following an effort to isolate the ensemble, Moiseyev founded his own dance company, which brought together dancers in a professional ensemble whose quality was comparable to the ballet dancers of the Bolshoi Theatre.

Moiseyev, Hernandez, Reda, and other choreographers lived in an atmosphere in which the urban man regarded the peasants as dirty, busy and uneducated. The

---

15 Zálešák, *Folklórne hnutie na Slovensku*, 21–22.
16 In the broader sense, folklore ballet is scenically transformed folk dance, which is interpreted by the folk dance ensemble onstage. This new kind of stage dance art was created by three Soviet ensembles in the 1930s. The folk dance of socialist countries, from the GDR and the Korean People's Democratic Republic to the Democratic Republic of Vietnam, lived a true Renaissance (Rebling, 1986, s. 32).
17 Shay, *Choreographic Politics: State Folk Dance Companies, Representation and Power*, 67.

artistic production of this part of the population had to be altered, purified and "improved" for the eyes and senses of modern middle-class audiences in major cities. Because of this, choreographers during training turned to what was (and still is) considered to be the best form of art – ballet and modern dance, which were the basis of their dance training.[18]

Dance analysis of Moiseyev's ballet shows that Igor Moiseyev in his choreographic works used character dance, a subdivision of classical dance, which he changed and perfected into a unique movement vocabulary, hence "his attempt was to create a perfect folk dance".[19]

The staging of folk dance in Slovakia after World War II
Initial period 1948–1955[20]

A characteristic feature of the initial period was the expansion of music and dance folklore in stage interpretations. The main representatives were folklore groups and folklore ensembles. As folklore groups were directly linked to their own local dance, vocal and musical tradition, urban, factory and school ensembles imitated, reconstructed and stylized folklore.[21]

As mentioned above, the impetus for the formation of folklore groups in the former Czechoslovakia was similar to the collectives in the Soviet Union who came to visit the country with inimitable artistic performances immediately after the end of World War II and the communist takeover in February 1948. The initiators of the formation and the first leaders of folklore ensembles were mostly local teachers and other enthusiasts of different professions and vocation.[22]

---

18 Shay, *Choreographic Politics: State Folk Dance Companies, Representation and Power*, 32–33.

19 Shay, *Choreographic Politics: State Folk Dance Companies, Representation and Power*, 70.

20 Based on the basic division of the stages of the folklore movement in C. Zálešák's *The Folklore Movement in Slovakia* (1982) and E. T. Bartko's *The Styles of Slovak Dance Art* 1920–2010 (2011); however, they are slightly modified on the basis of new knowledge gained by the study of the literature.

21 Zálešák, *Folklórne hnutie na Slovensku*, 16.

22 Zálešák, *Folklórne hnutie na Slovensku*, 21–22.

As a result of the political changes following the so-called Victorious February of 1948,[23] the state ordered centralized management of all sectors, including culture. Attention was drawn to the manifestations of folk culture and folklore that were to be developed in folklore ensembles. While other expressions of folk-art were considered to be reproductive art, folklore ensembles were required to continue with their tradition and produce new folk songs, games, dances and fairy tales: "Today, if we want to continue in these traditions, we need to create a similar environment. We organize works in folk dance ensembles so that their artistic activities are attended by the masses working in factories, towns and villages. In addition to stage performances, dance groups should direct their activities to promoting and organizing mass folk dance and folk songs at their workplace".[24]

The unrealistic requirement to "produce" folklore through folk ensembles led to their extraordinary increase in number during the first half of the 1950s. They were categorized as children's, pioneer, youth, student, factory, military, railway ensembles etc. The leading representatives of the folk movement were, however, the two most important ensembles, the Slovak National Folklore Ballet Lúčnica and the Slovak State Traditional Dance Company, SĽUK. Their professional performances became a model for the amateur folklore movement in their manner of producing music and dance compositions, and the popularity of formal effects, dance interpretation and costumes:

> As far as choreographies are concerned, we tried to use authentic material, but then more or less things were influenced by me as a pedagogue, by SĽUK, Lúčnica, the State Ensemble [Czechoslovak State Ensemble of Song and Dance in Prague – author's note], the Russian ensembles. We wanted to do something like this. So, we've been doing something like that so we have to raise the level of the ensemble. Hints, diagonals and all sorts of bumps, runs, and bulls.[25]

---

23 Victorious February is the name of the communist coup in the Czechoslovakia, which took place between February 17 and February 25, 1948. Today it is perceived by non-communists as a transition from democracy to totalitarianism, affiliation to the Soviet bloc, the beginning of oppression and economic decline.

24 Zálešák, *Propagujeme nové metódy práce v súboroch ľudového tanca*, 40.

25 Hvižďák, 2014.

That was the model [the SĽUK and Lúčnica ensembles – author's note]. *Maybe the Alexandrov Ensemble and the Moiseyev Dance Company set an example to them. And, based on them, the folklore movement was oriented. Of course, that was the model. That was the trend! They showed how to do it on the stage. The Lúčnica ensemble was a total model for the amateur folklore movement. The SĽUK ensemble made mainly musical artistic productions.*[26]

As for the dance performances and choreographic strategies in the first years of folk dance performance (by Štefan Nosáľ at the Lúčnica ensemble and Juraj Kubánka in SĽUK ensemble), one cannot compare them to the higher forms of stylization that existed during their peak period of creation. Choreographers focused on the choreographic principle of the so-called fun in the village motif, using folk dance technique, not classical dance technique. Although they tended to dance in ranks facing the audience due to the way of performing folk dancing by Soviet ensembles, the dance style and the dance technique retained the identity of folk dance.

During this period, the prestigious and popular *Youth Creativity Competition*, a system of competitions featuring various artistic activities (including folk groups), took place from 1948. The folklore ensembles and folk groups competed with each other on the tour, but the folklore ensembles always targeted better performance and had higher artistic aims, whereas folk groups were rarely successful in the competition. The set rules influenced the quality of the performances negatively, as competition led the ensembles and groups to formalized effects in choreographies.[27]

In addition to *Folk Artistic Creativity Competitions*, folklore collectives were represented at folklore festivals. The oldest and most important is the Východná Folk Festival, which originated in 1953 at the instigation of members of the folk group from Východná village after their experience of performing at the folklore festival in Strážnica. In the first years of the festival, collectives from the nearby surroundings were represented, and from 1956, the festival had the character of an all-Slovak performance of authentic and stylized folklore.

---

26 Kovačovič, 2015.
27 Zálešák, *Folklórne hnutie na Slovensku*, 125–127.

The staging of folk dance in Slovakia between 1956 and 1969

The significant quantitative increase in amateur ensembles at an inadequate qualitative level and their very frequent representation at social events resulted in a wide-scale debate among professionals around the need for such ensembles and their place in society in 1958. The first impetus for the debate was the contribution of Vladimír Mináč's, *The Weight of Folklore* (Literary Newspaper,[28] 1958, No. 12), in which he deeply criticizes the development of the folklore movement in the then Czechoslovakia, but especially the way society tolerated the insufficient quality level of the SĽUK ensemble:

> Unfortunately, the truth is, on the other hand, that the new premiere of the SĽUK ensemble does not bear witness to a further rise, but to the slow and permanent decline of this ensemble; new partisan dance is not another success; it has nothing to do with art, neither with folk art nor with the Slovak national uprising. It is a galimatyas, composed of the musical motifs of East Slavonic csardas, of some choreographic elements of the partisan dance of the Alexandrov ensemble, and a hint of a naive story; the result of this mix is operetta kitsch.[29]

There was a wave of responses in the form of similar contributions, gradually published mainly in the journal Cultural Life[30] (1958). Negative criticism was mainly due to the manner of creation of the new folklore ensembles through their significant increase in number over a very short period: "There have been some thoughts that what ensembles produced and still produce as songs and dances is folklore. Reason and satisfaction was then: there is nothing to worry about contemporary folk creativity, we have a lot of ensembles, and then the current folklore works will bloom".[31]

The great wave of criticism affected the SĽUK and Lúčnica ensembles' programs and performances, because amateur ensembles began to take over the process of creating and working in ensembles without well-trained leaders and choreographers. The second objection generally found

---

28 Literární noviny.
29 Mináč, *Tíha folklóru*, 1.
30 Kultúrny život.
31 Michálek, *Za hlboké poznanie folklórnej tvorby nášho ľudu*, 6.

in the above-mentioned contributions concerned the artistic orientation of the SĽUK and Lúčnica ensembles:

> These ensembles [SĽUK and Lúčnica ensembles – author's note] achieved enough of their original mission very quickly: seeking, pulling out of the real jewels of folk art, clearing them from falsity, and thus displaying them perfectly in the classic form today. But it was then decided and easy to accept that SĽUK and Lúčnica ensembles in particular had not only to draw on folk art but to "develop" and "enrich" it, and thus to return it to the people.[32]
>
> The results of such work emerged soon: for example, many promising evolving song and dance ensembles began to perceive their great role models, imitate them, and follow all sorts of "instructional-methodical" instructions to "consolidate" their methods. Somewhere here one of the reasons for the present exaggeration of folklore is, if true, it is still about folklore.[33]

Notwithstanding these negatives, this period in the development of the folklore movement brought a significant increase in the form of competitions and tours. Many new folklore festivals were organized, as well as specialized competitions, by founding organizations or individual artistic unions. An important event for Slovak folklore ensembles was The Second Nationwide Spartakiad in Prague in 1960. In addition to this Spartakiad, there were organized another two in 1955 and 1965. The Spartakiads helped the development of folklore ensembles greatly, especially those who did not have experienced leaders. It represented an education in choreographic work and training methods for them. Emphasis was on the precise observance of established lines and patterns in which dance resembled a sporting activity more than an artistic one.

However, despite many events where folklore ensembles featured with their choreographies, their performances did not always reach a sufficient level of quality: "We did not know about choreography in the true sense of the word, the laws of the stage, the art form. The ensemble's leader considered choreography as the drawing of images on the stage, playing with various shapes and formations."[34]

Experts' contributions also mention other shortcomings in the choreographic creations of amateur ensembles: the superficiality in maintaining

---

32 Kaliský, *Folklór dnes*, 4.
33 Michálek, *Za hlboké poznanie folklórnej tvorby nášho ľudu*, 6.
34 Konopáska, *Od tradícií k dnešku: 15 rokov súborov piesní a tancov*, 210.

the regional purity of dances[35], the imitation of choreographies of professional ensembles[36], insufficient dance training of dancers in ensembles[37],
the pretense of the creation and stealing of the compositional elements
from other choreographers[38], banality, frivolity, cheap effects and means
of expression, inappropriately chosen costumes[39], inadequate originality of
dance-stage work, an indolent approach to choreographic work and tem-
plate techniques in the process of creating choreography. "The results of
such 'creativity' are The East, The Goral, The Cigáň (Gypsy), The Dupák
(Stamping), The Trenčín and The Kubra dances".[40,41] These dances were
the result of mixing the various elements of the regional culture without
an internal logical sequence and preserving their basic structural features.

The problems described were the result of a low level of knowledge of
choreography, ethno-choreology and dance pedagogy at that time, which
was also reflected upon by Slovak choreographers and folklorists:

> We also have a lack of professionally trained choreographers for song and dance
> ensembles and methodologists in educational institutions. Theoretical works in
> the field of dance are in diapers – de facto, there is not anyone who cares about
> the development of dance theory. There is a single researcher for the whole dance
> field who does not know whether he should be collecting and filming folk dances,
> or creating a dance classification system or dealing with dance history, or whether
> to explore contemporary choreographic works. Of course, the creation of a sci-
> ence of dance here cannot even be said to exist under these conditions.[42]

---

35 Zálešák, *Ideme správnym smerom?*, 60.
36 Zálešák, *Ideme správnou cestou?*, 85.
37 Kovačovič, *Ukážme si správnu cestu*, 210.
38 Dúžek, *Ide o tanečné súbory*, 179.
39 Jelínková, *Veľa diskutujeme?*, 118.
40 Ondrejka, *Nepomohla by tanečnej tvorbe väčšia nápaditosť?*, 138.
41 It was customary to name individual choreography according to the most char-
     acteristic feature of a dance (Dupák: the "Stamping" dance), specific ethnic
     group (Cigáň: the "Gypsy" dance), place (Trenčín: a Slovak town in the west
     of the country) or region (Východ: the "East" dance) where the dance comes
     from. The results were choreographies with mixed structural features, costumes
     that resembled only the basics of the original and a musical accompaniment that
     often changed only a few enriched songs.
42 Zálešák, *Problémy tanečného umenia*, 36.

The situation in leadership was inevitably reflected in the level of the training of leaders – the choreographers in the amateur folk movement. It is not surprising that the ensembles and their leaders chose an "easier" way:

> Instead of trying to teach old folk dances, knowing the folklore of our villages, they began to "stylize" and "choreograph" often only with two or three danced elements (to several overplayed folk songs), which they used in effective, but hollow shapes. Following the example of the SĽUK and Lúčnica ensembles, they sought to have a two-hour long programme, a large choir, orchestra, etc. Many of the choreographic works were lacking in many of these elements: good artwork, serious research, artistic leadership.[43]

A systemic error, based on the over-frequent scheduling of competitions during this period, forced leaders without sufficient professional training to change their repertoire annually. For amateur folk ensembles, it was practically impossible to meet this demand.

The staging of folk dance in Slovakia in the period 1970–1989

In the 1970s, nationwide multidisciplinary competitions of hobbyist artistic activity[44] were renewed, but only in the form of one-off events on the occasion of cultural-political anniversaries: "All these Czechoslovak and international festivals were primarily a manifestation of the idea of socialism and international co-operation".[45]

As in previous periods, the results and quality of the folklore movement in Slovakia reflected popular folklore festivals. In the 1970s and 1980s, the *Public Education Institute*[46] prepared three types of events to increase the professional growth of folklore ensembles: *The Czechoslovak Festival of Folklore Ensembles*[47] (1971, 1974, 1977 and 1980), *Ensembles' Performances of Quality*[48] (1976, 1979, 1982, 1985 and 1988) and *Slovak*

---

43 Zálešák, *Roztancovaná zem*, 362.
44 ZUČ – Záujmová umelecká činnosť (hobbyist artistic activity)
45 Zálešák, *Folklórne hnutie na Slovensku*, 143.
46 Osvetový ústav is a state contributory organization of the Ministry of Culture of the Slovak Republic, which performs the function of a national-professional workplace for cultural and educational activity.
47 Československý festival folklórnych súborov.
48 Kvalitatívne prehrávky folklórnych súborov.

Choreography Competition of Folklore Ensembles[49] (since 1978 held every three years).[50]

The main objective of the Czechoslovak Folklore Festival was to encourage the creation of thematic and direct combined programs. It was held every three years. Slovak ensembles showed great interest in participating in the competition. However, the effects of the isolation between Slovak and Czech ensembles in the folk movement were evident. While the performances of the Czech ensembles were of good quality both in terms of high culture, music, singing and dance performance, the Slovak ensembles excelled especially in advanced dance technique and dynamics of speech. Briefly, the Czech, Moravian and Slovak folklore ensembles had a different approach to the onstage re-evaluation of folklore.[51]

An important event also taking place triennially from 1976 was *The Ensembles' Performances of Quality*. The idea of establishing The Ensembles' Performances of Quality was born in the 1960s, but the logistically demanding and time-consuming event could not be realized until the second half of the 1970s (Zima, 1980, p. 10). The intent of The Ensembles´ Performances of Quality was to get an overview of the ability of the ensembles to prepare a separate feature program. Depending on the quality of the programs, the ensembles were then categorized as A and B or lower C and D. These events were organized in a three-year cycle, with each of the ensembles having to defend their position in the category. The events mobilized the ensembles to create choreographies, enhance the quality and balance of their programs, and offered inter-ensemble competition as a stimulus to raise their artistic level.[52]

The Ensembles' Performances of Quality also had the character of educational seminars. The jury that evaluated the performances gave the choreographer and team leaders valuable advice to improve their choreographic work. For many amateur choreographers, this was the main way to get new and up-to-date knowledge.

---

49 Choreografická súťaž folklórnych súborov.
50 Zálešák, *Folklórne hnutie na Slovensku*, 144.
51 Zálešák, *Folklórne hnutie na Slovensku*, 144–146.
52 Zálešák, *Folklórne hnutie na Slovensku*, 147–149.

The Ensembles' Performances of Quality began in the late 1970s. The entire process of The Performances inspired or somehow pushed the ensembles back to the original form of folk dances and to stage what they knew according to the original folklore material. At that time, the practice was that the ensembles in the 1960s and early 1970s did the "East" dance, the "Goral"[53] dance, the "Podpoľanie"[54] dance [...] there were absolutely no choreographies according to the origin of the competitor, according to the locality. The choreographer generally did the "East" dance.[55]

The *Slovak Choreography Competition of Folklore Ensembles* was created in 1978 to create an opportunity for the presentation of the most successful choreographies of folk ensembles. At the same time, new approaches to folklore were presented to support progressive choreographic streams. Several choreographic processes and various forms of styling of the dance material (from the reconstruction of original forms to choreographically demanding dramatic themes) emerged.[56]

During this period, there was a debate around the professional orientation of the folk movement not only in Slovakia, but also among Czech experts. The professional community may have noticed the need to direct the choreographic work of folk ensembles, which were still reluctant to believe in the fragmented views of the jurors of the competitions in the approach to folklore material, which, for many reasons, resulted in an unnecessarily poor imitation of folklore. The folklore festivals and competitions were the ideal setting for professional conferences including international participation to discuss topics that had been addressed intensely in the folk movement in Slovakia. The contextual focus of the conferences included practical and theoretical themes: the problems of the stage presentation of dance folklore, problems of choreographic work in folklore ensembles, the content and future development of folklore festivals, defining the functions of folklore ensembles, and defining the appropriate terminology in folkloristics.

---

53 The Goral are a specific ethnographic group in Slovakia whose members live in different villages in the Orava and Spiš region.
54 Podpoľanie is located in the central part of Slovakia. Its center is the town of Zvolen.
55 Urban, 2015.
56 Zálešák, *Folklórne hnutie na Slovensku*, 149–150.

In addition, the *Public Education Institute* in Bratislava began organizing the largest training program for leaders of non-professional folklore ensembles from all over Slovakia in the 1970s. Those interested in learning improved their knowledge of ethnology, choreography, field research methodology, folk dance pedagogy, folk clothing and stage choreography. The lecturers were respected experts: Cyril Zálešák (folk dance), Štefan Nosáľ (choreography), Juraj Kubánka (choreography), Kliment Ondrejka (folklore research), Viliam Gruska (stage design) and Alexander Móži (folk music).[57] The above-mentioned facts should have helped the amateur folklore movement to overcome its choreographic problems. During this period the following were mentioned: a low number of chamber choreographies and an absence of natural motif binding; modest, square and unnatural evolving spatial formations[58]; the symmetry of choreographies[59]; and an effort to effect, not respecting the form of dance[60].

At the end of this period, the stage presentation of folklore required local identification of the folklore material from which the stage presentation originated, emphasizing the need to return to original sources and realization of field research, highlighting the maturity and purity of dance, singing and musical interpretation.[61] This is concisely summarized in Jan Blaho's contribution in Rytmus magazine, which mentions the modern approach to teaching folk dance using available archive videos[62], highlighting the knowledge of folklore material before the choreographic work itself[63]. Regarding the degree of folklore stylization on stage, he notes that transcription of folklore material, the lowest degree of stylization, is necessary and should form the basis upon which it is possible to build and develop a masterpiece at a higher degree of stylization, rejecting the phenomenon

---

57 Zálešák, *Folklórne hnutie na Slovensku*, 74–75.
58 Zima, *Usmerňovať prácu folklórnych súborov*, 10–11.
59 Kyseľ, *Amatérske folklórne súbory v roku 1982*, 10–11.
60 Kyseľ, *Prehrávky folklórnych súborov*, 10–11.
61 Hamar, *Folklór v tieni scénického folklorizmu*, 215.
62 Blaho, *Premeny tanca – prenášanie tradičného ľudového tanca v súčasnom podmienkach*, s. 10–11.
63 Blaho, *Tradičné tance – základ práce amatérskych folklórnych súborov*, s. 14–15.

of "stylized stylization",[64] which apparently resonated in choreographic production of amateur folk ensembles in the second half of the 1980s[65]. He further emphasized the need for the wider and deeper knowledge of the choreographer in the folklore ensemble[66] and summarized the basic principles of stage folklore processing[67].

The staging of folk dance in Slovakia in the period 1990–1999

We can describe the last period very briefly. Rytmus magazine was closed in 1992, thus disrupting the existence of a professional forum to react promptly to the current events in the folk movement. The socio-political events of November 1989 brought fundamental changes to the life of folklore ensembles and the entire folk movement: On the one hand, the folklore movement is "liberated" from the unhealthy ideological pressures of one ruling party, on the other hand it is more or less subject to economic "pressure"[68]. Immediately after the revolution, the folk movement became the centerpiece of stereotypical ideas that did not serve the positive development of the situation.[69]

The new political establishment brought with it a number of positives and negatives: on the one hand, the undisputed positives of the grant system, sponsorship and commercial activity, but which, without transparent financing and advanced cultural policy, do not always mean promoting

---

64 Stylized stylization was a phenomenon appearing in choreographies of amateur folklore ensembles from the 1970s. It was associated with less talented and educated amateur choreographers and the strong influence of choreographic production of professional ensembles (especially the Lúčnica ensemble) on the choreographic creations of non-professional ensembles. It was manifested by the taking of stylized elements from choreographies of professional ensembles by choreographers of non-professional ensembles and using them in their own creations.

65 Blaho, *Štylizácia a miera štylizácie folklóru*, 18–19.

66 Blaho, *Scénické spracovanie ľudových tancov v amatérskych folklórnych súboroch – skúsenosti a úvahy choreografa*, 10–12.

67 Blaho, *Hlavné princípy a zásady scénického spracovania folklóru*, 17.

68 Hamar, *Folklór v tieni scénického folklorizmu*, 215.

69 Hamar, *Folklór v tieni scénického folklorizmu*, 216.

the highest quality production. This fact, however, Juraj Hamar, Associate Professor of the Department of Esthetics and current general director of SĽUK ensemble, attributes to the general phenomenon of the crisis of culture, to the collective decline of moral and esthetic criteria connected with the desacralization and demythologization of society.[70]

There is a need for new staging approaches in folklore that come with modern technologies (large-screen projection, light design, amplification). On the other hand, "only a few festivals plan their direction in the form of dramaturgical supervision several years ahead".[71]

Concerning choreographic work, positives include the partial elimination of theatrical clichés and gestures, and attempts to improvise and experiment with world music; but theatrical, spatial, motivational and dramaturgical clichés, and inadequate contact with original material still persist. The current debate is about authenticity, but it is not covered by expert discussion. In the artistic work of folk ensembles, profound knowledge (in all aspects related to folklore and folklore ecology) is accentuated during this period, with no regard for the notion of "when I love something, I do it well".[72]

Conclusion

With the birth of the Lúčnica ensemble, a new understanding of dance esthetics, especially in folklore ensembles, arrived into the development of stage forms of folk art. By 1948, folklore groups mainly presented onstage, using the lowest forms of stylization in their performances.

After the end of World War II, a development in the stage expression of folk culture took place in all the socialist states of the Eastern Bloc. In 1948, almost immediately after the war, the Moiseyev Dance Company came to Czechoslovakia to present their art, which for a long time changed the view of folk culture in our ensembles. The technique of classical dance was implemented in the stage interpretation of folk dance, which underwent a general change in the perception of the esthetics of stage folk dance.

70 Hamar, *Folklór v tieni scénického folklorizmu*, 216.
71 Hamar, *Folklór v tieni scénického folklorizmu*, 218.
72 Hamar, *Folklór v tieni scénického folklorizmu*, 219.

Firstly, the professional ensembles SĽUK and Lúčnica were affected, and later on, following their lead, other amateur ensembles. Lúčnica and SĽUK, however, had trained dance pedagogues and conditions for the technical handling of demanding dance routines. In some amateur ensembles, unfortunately, the effort to mimic the performances of professional dancers appeared comical.

The situation was so alarming that in the 1970s, the professional community began to systematically address stage folklorism via theoretical aspects, as well as providing professional support to non-professional folk ensembles. The result was the theoretical clarification of problems associated with choreographic work, but only their partial application in practice.

In the 1990s, the situation changed slightly with the arrival of a new generation of choreographers working with choreographer Ervín Varga, influenced by the Hungarian dance folk movement. Košice and Bratislava became the centers of new choreographic work. The analysis of this period does not fall into the scope to which the study was devoted and will be discussed in later papers.

Denis Svetlák

Significant nurses and their activities in the Slovak National Uprising

Abstract: This study deals with the so far little known and explored chapter of the course of the Slovak National Uprising. It describes the activities of nurses as active participants in the uprising. These little-known women provided the necessary treatment for the wounded partisans, providing health care during and after the fighting. In addition to opening a topic that has so far been at the margins of interest in Slovak historiography, the study also introduces an element of gender studies on the topic of national history, which is traditionally viewed through political and military-strategic aspects. It consists of 9 biographical medallions, which represent a chronological description across the lives of these little-known characters of armed uprising against the regime of the Slovak state.

Keywords: nurses, war, uprising, Slovakia, Red cross, Slovak state

Authors of monographs, studies and articles usually focus on the description of individual army branches in dealing with World War II. These usually comprise three basic branches: naval, air and ground forces. They also concentrate on the individual facets of armaments and equipment, number of personnel or prototypes of weapons and machines developed to improve a position in a given military conflict. However, they often forget about the people – the ordinary regulars who form these three basic branches. It is they who fight on the front line, use and operate individual machines and machinery. It is mainly regulars, members of units consisting of ordinary men and less frequently women, who form the core of every single army and who undertake the highest risk of injury or in the worst case, loss of their own lives. Injury and death are undoubtedly the features of the bloodiest and most tragic conflict of the 20th century – World War II.

There were many casualties on both sides during World War II. It was necessary to remove them from the battlefield to a safe place, give them first aid, proper medical care as well as provide them with medicine, bandages and even food. This praiseworthy activity was mainly done by women working as nurses. These women were undoubtedly very devoted, not to mention courageous. Not much is known about the women who helped in the Slovak National Uprising. Their assistance in individual battles has unjustly been forgotten. Every single one of these women was exceptional in her unselfishness, courage and devotion. That is why every woman deserves special attention. Nurses and their activities played a very important role in the Slovak National Uprising that should not be forgotten.

Individual archives provide a considerably large amount of information about the women who served during the Slovak National Uprising as nurses. However, when exploring the research on this period, it seemed that these women had been forgotten. In the case of monographs, there is not a large amount of information concerning nurses during the Slovak National Uprising. Most books about the Slovak National Uprising focus on individual battles, organization, revolt or significant figures, such as generals. However, it is necessary to point out the women in the role of nurses who saved a considerable number of lives thanks to their activities. In writing this work, I mainly used archive sources which provided me with a sufficient amount of relevant information. This chapter consists of biographies of the women who were among the most significant nurses in the Slovak National Uprising.

Mária Bíziková

Her maiden name was Mária Gavroňská. She was born on October 25, 1921, in a part of Ružomberok called Rybárpole. She took part in the Slovak National Uprising as a nurse of the Red Cross.[12] The hospital in Ružomberok[3] became her first workplace; later she worked in a field

---

1   *Životopis Márie Bízikovej.* Archive of the Ministry of Interior of SR – Military historical archive, *Profesionálne a sociálne skupiny v SNP,* file Živena, Drobová, *Životopisy žien – Účastníčok SNP,* 3.

2   The Red Cross played a very important role in the Slovak National Uprising. It organized medical help on battle lines and provided medical care in rebel-held territory. Junas et al., *80 rokov Červeného kríža na Slovensku,* 51.

3   The military hospital in Ružomberok was the only military hospital that operated in rebel-held territory. They gradually started to establish field hospitals and other alternative health care facilities. Junas et al., *80 rokov,* 51.

hospital in Korytnica.[4] Then she worked as a nurse in the medical service of the 1st Czechoslovak army corps.[5] She received many awards for her creditable activities: the Highest Award of the International Red Cross; the Florence Nightingale Medal[6]; the State Award for Credit for Development; a silver and gold medal For Devoted and Meritorious Work in the Czechoslovak Red Cross; she is also a holder of the Bronze Janského Plaque, commemorative medals of the Slovak National Uprising as well as the Honorary Badge of Association of Anti-fascist Fighters.[7]

However, her life story is much more important than her collection of awards. She had become a member of the Red Cross before she finished medical school. The hospital in Ružomberok which had been founded around 1914 became her first workplace during the war. Wounded soldiers from the eastern front were brought to this place during World War I. Her first patients were men who had been injured in Poland. There were mainly Polish soldiers who were wounded in battles with German units. The hospital in Ružomberok had come under military supervision within a short period. Moreover, it was frequently checked by the fascists. Mária Bíziková started helping actively at a relatively early age. It all started with a blood donation when she was 17 – she donated the life-saving fluid to a wounded Polish aviator. Her activities against the regime started to develop afterwards. She helped several recovered men to escape from the hospital, mainly by means of bringing civilian clothes which enabled these men to leave the hospital without being noticed. Doctors from the hospital in Ružomberok helped her in this activity as well. They had even more

---

4   Korytnica is situated in the district of Ružomberok and is famous for its mineral water. Source: Mulík, *Dejiny kúpeľov a kúpeľníctva na Slovensku*, 156, 166.

5   The medical service of the first Czechoslovak army corps was founded at the beginning of the Slovak National Uprising. It was led by MUDr. Štefan Darvaš and MUDr. Ján Paškan. It cooperated with rebellious Slovak National Council and together they reorganized all hospitals and spas situated on the territory of rebels into military ones. Junas et al., *80 rokov*, 51.

6   An English nurse known also as "the lady with the lamp". She founded the first school for nurses in the world. Source: Carpenter, *Health, Medicine, and Society in Victorian England*, 167.

7   *Životopis Márie Bízikovej*. Archive of the Ministry of Interior of SR – Military historical archive, *Profesionálne a sociálne skupiny v SNP*, file Živena, Drobová, *Životopisy žien – Účastníčok* SNP, 3.

opportunities in which to help these men – creating various false diagnoses, putting healthy limbs into plaster to prevent these men from being deported to concentration camps. Mária Bíziková was also a witness to these procedures. In cooperation with the doctors, medical staff and local inhabitants of Rybárpole, she managed to help 33 Polish soldiers to escape the hospital in Ružomberok. Not only Mária Bíziková, but also the local inhabitants brought civilian clothes and provided shelter to recovered Polish soldiers. The hospital in Ružomberok started to become more and more crowded. There were mainly men wounded on the eastern front and members of banned organizations who were engaged in activities against the regime. Mária Bíziková was among the few people who knew about the members of banned organizations who were being treated and recovering in this hospital. These members of banned organizations were assigned false names which provided them with the necessary cover during their treatment. She treated various injuries, some of which had been caused by mines or grenades. Patients who came to her were often deaf as a result of injury. During unannounced inspections by regime supporters, she had to calm down these patients so that they did not give themselves away via shouting caused by pain from various injuries.[8]

After the Slovak National Uprising broke out, she became a nurse in the service of the rebels. Her workplace moved to a field hospital in Korytnica.[9] She helped with the physical transportation of the wounded, which was quite difficult for a woman. It required a lot of effort to load wounded men much heavier than her. Thanks to her determination she was able to save and treat several hundred wounded rebels. During this period she was a witness to several tragic events, including an attack on a medical convoy by the Germans. These attacks resulted in an increased number of wounded and dead. Nurses struggled to take those who had

8   *Životopis Márie Bízikovej.* Archive of the Ministry of Interior of SR – Military historical archive, *Profesionálne a sociálne skupiny v SNP*, file Živena, Drobová, *Životopisy žien – Účastníčok SNP*, 3.
9   The military hospital in Ružomberok had to be evacuated due to the retreat of partisans. It was moved and divided into two workplaces: a newly opened Field Hospital 1 in Korytnica and Field Hospital 2 in Tisovec. Junas et al., *80 rokov*, 51.

survived out of numerous ambulances which were on fire. They tried hard to get the rescued to safety and treat them again.[10]

The end of the war was the most difficult period for Mária Bíziková. As the Slovak National Uprising was suppressed, a period of terror came. The Gestapo started to check civilians as well as medical staff. These checks lacked any relevant procedure of investigation. Many civilians and medical staff were accused of being members of partisan units without any proof. They were randomly chosen and then either shot or transported to concentration camps. Mária Bíziková was also put in a prison run by the Gestapo. She was questioned in a brutal fashion that included torture. She had wounds on her body and damaged hearing as a result of what she experienced. Maria went grey at quite an early age. It is very likely that it was the result of the horror she had experienced during the war and especially in prison. She was also a witness to the beating of a pregnant woman who died as a consequence of her injuries.[11]

In 1945, Mária Bíziková managed to flee to the other side of the front thanks to the support of the Red Cross. Despite reaching relative safety, she did not stop working as a nurse. The medical service of the first Czechoslovak corps became the last place where she worked as a nurse.[12]

Mária Flešková

Her maiden name was Mária Bobáľová. She was born on August 31, 1922 in Lovinobaňa. She was a member of the Red Cross and worked in the hospital in Lovinobaňa. She significantly helped partisans mainly in the surroundings of the Dobročské and Kotmanovské forests. She received a lot of awards and commemorative medals for her participation in the Slovak National Uprising, as well as a Medal for Devoted and Meritorious

---

10 *Životopis Márie Bízikovej*. Archive of the Ministry of Interior of SR – Military historical archive, *Profesionálne a sociálne skupiny v SNP*, file Živena, Drobová, *Životopisy žien – Účastníčok SNP*, 3.

11 *Životopis Márie Bízikovej*. Archive of the Ministry of Interior of SR – Military historical archive, *Profesionálne a sociálne skupiny v SNP*, file Živena, Drobová, *Životopisy žien – Účastníčok SNP*, 3.

12 *Životopis Márie Bízikovej*. Archive of the Ministry of Interior of SR – Military historical archive, *Profesionálne a sociálne skupiny v SNP*, file Živena, Drobová, *Životopisy žien – Účastníčok SNP*, 3.

Work for the Czechoslovak Red Cross of the first class. She was also the holder of a departmental honor of the Ministry of Health of the Slovak Socialist Republic and a J.G. Gwoth Medal. The Florence Nightingale Medal went on to become undoubtedly her highest award.[13]

Mária Flešková found herself in a complicated situation during the Slovak National Uprising. Július Fleško,[14] a member of the Slovak National Uprising, became her husband. He took part in battles in the surroundings of Telgárt. Mária stayed at home with her little son who still needed care at that time. Her parents provided her with support and help. Despite the complicated situation she decided to become a volunteer nurse for the Red Cross. She did a nursing course organized by said organization.[15] Then she started work at the military hospital in Lovinobaňa. As she took care of her child during the day, she worked mainly at night.[16]

Later she started to supply rebels in the surroundings of the Kotmanovské and Dobročské forests with medical supplies. She had to deal with difficult terrain and unfavorable weather during the transport of these supplies. She was a witness of and participant in the necessary evacuation of the hospital in Lovinobaňa. As the German units came closer and gradually pushed the rebels back, worries about the lives of the wounded in the hospital started to increase. The wounded were gradually moved to shelters in the surrounding woods as their safety was in question. Mária Flešková tried to help with the moving of the wounded and took as many medical supplies as she could from the hospital in Lovinobaňa. As she was a member of the Red Cross, she had greater freedom in the territory occupied by Germans or members of the Hlinka Guard. Her activities were not only limited to nursing. When moving in enemy territory, she took notice of military units, their movement and everything that could be helpful to

13 *Životopis Márie Fleškovej*. Archive of the Ministry of Interior of SR – Military historical archive, *Profesionálne a sociálne skupiny v SNP*, file Živena, Drobová, *Životopisy žien – Účastníčok SNP*, 11.
14 Cséfalvay et al., *Vojenské osobnosti dejín Slovenska 1939–1945*, 66.
15 The Red Cross organized annual basic courses intended for women who wanted to become voluntary nurses. Junas et al., *80 rokov*, 47.
16 *Životopis Márie Fleškovej*. Archive of the Ministry of Interior of SR – Military historical archive, *Profesionálne a sociálne skupiny v SNP*, file Živena, Drobová,*Životopisy žien – Účastníčok SNP*, 11.

the rebels in the above-mentioned Kotmanovské and Dobročské forests. She provided information mainly to the headquarters of the partisan first Czechoslovak brigade of J.V. Stalin. Her work during the Slovak National Uprising was undoubtedly useful not only for the wounded, but also for the partisan units which were informed about enemy movements thanks to her. Mária Flešková learned about the end of the war in her native Lovinobaňa.[17]

Terézia Gulyášová

She was born on July 31, 1927 in Čierny Balog. During the Slovak National Uprising she was a member of a partisan brigade called Za slobodu Slovanov (For the Freedom of the Slavs).[18] She worked there as a nurse. Terézia Gulyášová received many awards for her activities: the Golden Star of Captain Nálepka; the Award of Meritorious Fighter against Fascism of the second class and a commemorative medal for the 20th anniversary of the Slovak National Uprising.[19]

She lost her mother when she was 11. Her life was undoubtedly difficult also due to this fact. On the other hand, it helped her to become a strong woman, which was proved by her activities during the Slovak National Uprising. A lot of young people from Čierny Balog joined the partisans during the Slovak National Uprising. Terézia Gulyášová joined the rebellion at the age of 17, thanks to the influence of her friends. Her friend Pavla Donovalová, who had joined the partisans before, supported her in her decision. Terézia took part in training in Valaská, where she learnt to handle weapons as well as the basics of nursing care taught by a certain doctor named Ferjancová. Terézia Gulyášová and her friend Pavla

17 *Životopis Márie Fleškovej*. Archive of the Ministry of Interior of SR – Military historical archive, *Profesionálne a sociálne skupiny v SNP*, file Živena, Drobová, *Životopisy žien – Účastníčok SNP*, 11.
18 *Životopis Márie Fleškovej*. Archive of the Ministry of Interior of SR – Military historical archive, *Profesionálne a sociálne skupiny v SNP*, file Živena, Drobová, *Životopisy žien – Účastníčok SNP*, 11.
19 *Životopis Terézie Gulyášovej*. Archive of the Ministry of Interior of SR – Military historical archive, *Profesionálne a sociálne skupiny v SNP*, file Živena, Ťapajová, *Životopisy žien – Účastníčok SNP*, 27.

Donovalová were assigned to the division of Peter Černov on the orders of Jevgenij Pavlovič Valjanskij, the commander of the brigade Za slobodu Slovanov (For the Freedom of the Slavs). She took part in numerous battles in many significant locations such as Čertovica, Boca, Malužiná, Porúbka, Liptovský Mikuláš, Kráľova Lehota and Važec. She participated in the fighting that erupted in Žiar nad Hronom, as well as in military and diversionary operations in the surroundings of Belice. She was also at the siege at Močiar, which she managed to escape together with her unit, and she took part in fighting at Dobrá Niva. She worked in the partisan division not only as a nurse, but also as a cook and helper with the transport of weapons and other materials. At the beginning of 1945, she helped with the transport of three wounded Soviet soldiers to partisan units. She experienced the last battles in her birthplace of Čierny Balog where the units of the Red Army came on January 29, 1945. After the war she worked in the hospital in Brezno as an assistant.[20]

Júlia Katrušinová

She was born on March 17, 1922 in Ľubietová. Her maiden name was Júlia Kmeťová. During the Slovak National Uprising she worked as a nurse of the first division of the Jánošík partisan brigade. She received commemorative medals on the anniversaries of the Slovak National Uprising and the Award of Meritorious Fighter of the Communist Party.[21]

Before starting to be active in anti-regime activities, she had worked as a servant. Her life changed after she met Július Majer, who belonged to the local communists of Ľubietová. He was active in supplying partisans hiding in the woods. He organized mainly young local boys for this activity but he recruited Júlia Kmeťová, too. Suppliers wanted to have better cover and therefore Júlia would go to the woods accompanied by a boy who was also a supplier. They wanted to create the impression that they were

---

20 *Životopis Terézie Gulyášovej.* Archive of the Ministry of Interior of SR – Military historical archive, *Profesionálne a sociálne skupiny v SNP*, file Živena, Ťapajová, *Životopisy žien – Účastníčok SNP*, 27.
21 *Životopis Júlie Katrušinovej.* Archive of the Ministry of Interior of SR – Military historical archive, *Profesionálne a sociálne skupiny v SNP*, file Živena, Burajová, *Životopisy žien – Účastníčok SNP*, 39.

a couple in love that had decided to go for a romantic walk. In fact, they were both going to partisans with supplies which were supposed to help them survive the difficult conditions caused by living in the woods.[22]

Activities with the aim of weakening the regime or supplying hiding partisans started to play an increasingly significant role in Júlia's life. However, the risk of being revealed was higher. Júlia became involved in various activities such as delivering leaflets, displaying posters of an anti-regime character and delivering messages. She was even more active in supporting partisans in 1944 after doing a medical course in Martin. She returned from there on August 7, 1944, and her first case was just around the corner. On the same day, she heard about a wounded Soviet doctor in Latiborská hoľa close to Ľubietová. She was a paratrooper who had been injured during landing.[23]

Her involvement in the Slovak National Uprising started at its outbreak. Together with her father, Ján Katrušin, she joined the Jánošík brigade[24] led by Ernest Bielik.[25] Júlia was in the first division, which was supposed to keep Národná street in Banská Bystrica under rebel control. When partisan units were marching down this street, a firefight broke out which left several wounded. Júlia treated her first wounded in this street.[26]

Her location changed on September 4, 1944. She was moved together with her division to Telgárt. Several gun battles between rebel units and Germans took place in the surroundings of this town. The rebels were attacked by the first German tank brigade which was armed with better equipment and weapons. Telgárt became known as the Slovak Stalingrad due to these battles. Júlia treated the wounded and she also helped

---

22 *Životopis Júlie Katrušinovej*. Archive of the Ministry of Interior of SR – Military historical archive, *Profesionálne a sociálne skupiny v SNP*, file Živena, Burajová, *Životopisy žien – Účastníčok SNP*, 39.

23 *Životopis Júlie Katrušinovej*. Archive of the Ministry of Interior of SR – Military historical archive, *Profesionálne a sociálne skupiny v SNP*, file Živena, Burajová, *Životopisy žien – Účastníčok SNP*, 39.

24 Plevza, *Dejiny Slovenského národného povstania 1944*, 444.

25 Lacko, *Slovenské národné povstanie 1944*, 141.

26 *Životopis Júlie Katrušinovej*. Archive of the Ministry of Interior of SR – Military historical archive, *Profesionálne a sociálne skupiny v SNP*, file Živena, Burajová, *Životopisy žien – Účastníčok SNP*, 39.

a woman give birth during the campaign. As the defensive position of the rebels started to be compromised, they received a command to retreat to the village of Spišské Mlynky on September 21. Rebel units were supposed to occupy the valley and organize offensive operations against approaching German units. After the partisans arrived in this area, they placed their wounded in individual houses.[27]

Júlia was given the task of getting medical supplies and was sent to Dobšiná. Six men who were supposed to obtain other supplies joined her. Ján Katrušin, who was a commander of the first division of Jánošík partisan brigade, also went to Dobšiná. He was supposed to meet there with several other commanders and agree on the coordination of their forces and subsequent procedure. Their stay in Dobšiná was prolonged by three days. When they came back, they met their fellow fighters who told them that their base in Spišské Mlynky had been attacked by German units that outnumbered them. A direct confrontation was impossible, which is why the partisan units had started to retreat again.[28]

On the next day they learnt that the German units had retreated from Spišské Mlynky. Júlia Katrušinová and other partisans wanted to find out what had happened to the wounded in Spišské Mlynky. When they entered the area, the atmosphere appeared very strange, as if it had been deserted.[29]

A curious event occurred right after they entered Spišské Mlynky. A soldier, whom they were not able to identify, started to shout at partisans entering the village in Russian: "Stop, drop your weapons!"[30] At first they were not sure if it was an ally or not. All doubts disappeared when they

---

27 *Životopis Júlie Katrušinovej.* Archive of the Ministry of Interior of SR – Military historical archive, *Profesionálne a sociálne skupiny v SNP*, file Živena, Burajová, *Životopisy žien – Účastníčok SNP*, 39.

28 *Životopis Júlie Katrušinovej.* Archive of the Ministry of Interior of SR – Military historical archive, *Profesionálne a sociálne skupiny v SNP*, file Živena, Burajová, *Životopisy žien – Účastníčok SNP*, 39.

29 *Životopis Júlie Katrušinovej.* Archive of the Ministry of Interior of SR – Military historical archive, *Profesionálne a sociálne skupiny v SNP*, file Živena, Burajová, *Životopisy žien – Účastníčok SNP*, 39.

30 *Životopis Júlie Katrušinovej.* Archive of the Ministry of Interior of SR – Military historical archive, *Profesionálne a sociálne skupiny v SNP*, file Živena, Burajová, *Životopisy žien – Účastníčok SNP*, 39.

heard the next command, this time in German. A firefight ensued. Ján Katrušin started to run away to the other platoon. Júlia found herself in the crossfire and saved her life at the last minute when she jumped through a window of one of the houses.[31]

She found an old woman in the house who was sitting there in the kitchen and covering her ears from the gunfire. She noticed Júlia after some time and hid her in a hole close to the stove. Then she covered the hole with a wooden plank and various objects. By evening Júlia began to panic at what had happened and did not know how the firefight had ended. She decided to run to the woods. However, she was caught by enemy units.[32]

Germans created a human shield from the captives whom they were pushing in front of themselves. Júlia assumed that she would be transported together with the captives to a concentration camp or executed somewhere in the woods. The enemy units were heading to Spišská Nová Ves. The transportation did not go smoothly and the German units were attacked by partisans. Júlia and several partisans took advantage of the chaos which broke out and escaped. She ran to a dam which was full of water at that time and hid there for several hours.[33]

Some partisans who knew Júlia assumed that she had been shot dead during her escape. That is why they informed her mother that she had been killed in battle. This turned out to be a mistake when after an exhausting walk Júlia Katrušinová appeared in Kráľova hoľa where her fellow fighters greeted her with surprise.[34]

---

31 *Životopis Júlie Katrušinovej.* Archive of the Ministry of Interior of SR – Military historical archive, *Profesionálne a sociálne skupiny v SNP*, file Živena, Burajová, *Životopisy žien – Účastníčok SNP*, 39.

32 *Životopis Júlie Katrušinovej.* Archive of the Ministry of Interior of SR – Military historical archive, *Profesionálne a sociálne skupiny v SNP*, file Živena, Burajová, *Životopisy žien – Účastníčok SNP*, 39.

33 *Životopis Júlie Katrušinovej.* Archive of the Ministry of Interior of SR – Military historical archive, *Profesionálne a sociálne skupiny v SNP*, file Živena, Burajová, *Životopisy žien – Účastníčok SNP*, 39.

34 *Životopis Júlie Katrušinovej.* Archive of the Ministry of Interior of SR – Military historical archive, *Profesionálne a sociálne skupiny v SNP*, file Živena, Burajová, *Životopisy žien – Účastníčok SNP*, 39.

Kráľova hoľa was the last test set for her by the war. There were shepherd's huts which the partisans used as their new shelters. The conditions were very harsh due to the inhospitable and freezing weather which came with autumn. They could not even warm themselves up by fires as they might be discovered by the enemy. Moreover, the partisan units also lacked supplies, mainly food. That is why Júlia and her fellow fighters tried to get supplies in surrounding villages. During this stay in Kráľova hoľa, the partisans managed to kidnap several enemy officers who were celebrating New Year's Eve at that time in Pohorelá. The end of war was close but they lacked food and it was still more and more difficult to get some. The lack of food, medical supplies as well as ammunition made their difficult situation even harder. They even found a source of meat in horses. Their salvation from the tragic situation came together with the units of the Red Army. Júlia Katrušinová was undoubtedly a very admirable woman. She could cope with the cruelest hardship. This was proved by her determination, unselfishness and resilience.[35]

Viera Malatová

Her maiden name was Viera Čunderlíková. She was born on February 3, 1922 in the hamlet of Rybô situated close to Banská Bystrica. Her work during the Slovak National Uprising included several activities. At first, she helped partisan units in various ways. Then she became a nurse in the first Czechoslovak partisan brigade of A. S. Jegorov.[36] Later she also worked in a brigade called Smrť fašizmu (Death to Fascism). Viera Malatová received the following awards: Meritorious Fighter against Fascism and Red Star of Member of Jegorov Brigade.[37]

---

35 *Životopis Júlie Katrušinovej*. Archive of the Ministry of Interior of SR – Military historical archive, *Profesionálne a sociálne skupiny v SNP*, file Živena, Burajová, *Životopisy žien – Účastníčok* SNP, 39.

36 *Životopis Viery Malatovej*. Archive of the Ministry of Interior of SR – Military historical archive, *Profesionálne a sociálne skupiny v SNP*, file Živena, Burajová, *Životopisy žien – Účastníčok* SNP, 59.

37 *Životopis Viery Malatovej*. Archive of the Ministry of Interior of SR – Military historical archive, *Profesionálne a sociálne skupiny v SNP*, file Živena, Burajová, *Životopisy žien – Účastníčok* SNP, 59.

She came from a large family – she had five siblings. She had had to cope with difficult conditions since childhood. She lost her father when she was a child. Her mother had to deal with considerable economic difficulties. She was forced to put two of her daughters in an orphanage in Radvaň. Viera Čunderlíková was one of them. When she was 14, she left the orphanage and came back to her mother and tried to support the family.[38]

Her mother, who found herself in a highly difficult situation, started to support the partisans. She gave them food and the clothes of her deceased husband. At first Viera Čunderlíková helped the partisans in a very similar way to her mother. She supplied them with food and clothes. In winter, the partisans used to go for supplies to nearby houses, but in spring and summer it was more difficult. Increased activity of enemy patrols prevented partisans from going to nearby houses as they were usually guarded. Ordinary citizens who brought supplies to partisans in the mountains were more active in these months. Viera Čunderlíková also took part in these activities. One such expedition took place on October 27, 1943. The group was supposed to meet partisans at Kráľova studňa and bring them supplies. When they reached this place, they found only one partisan there who told them to take the food to a different place – to Račianska dolina. This journey was replete with difficulties. First they had to cope with unfavorable weather, when it started to rain. They also found out that Turecká had been burnt down. Due to the unceasing downpour they decided to look for shelter until the weather improved. They went to Blatnická dolina which seemed to be the most suitable and closest option. On seeing one of the huts in this area, they found out that it was a military hospital founded by partisans. One of the nurses noticed that there was a woman on this expedition – Viera Čunderlíková. She had not even managed to dry herself properly before she started to help the nurse in the hospital.[39]

---

38 *Životopis Viery Malatovej.* Archive of the Ministry of Interior of SR – Military historical archive, *Profesionálne a sociálne skupiny v SNP*, file Živena, Burajová, *Životopisy žien – Účastníčok SNP*, 59.

39 *Životopis Viery Malatovej.* Archive of the Ministry of Interior of SR – Military historical archive, *Profesionálne a sociálne skupiny v SNP*, file Živena, Burajová, *Životopisy žien – Účastníčok SNP*, 59.

Shouts warning of approaching enemy units were heard at dawn. There was no possibility of evacuation as these units were very close to the hospital. When the enemy units arrived, all those who had not managed to escape or had not been able to escape because of their injuries were taken captive. All captives, including the wounded, had to manage a long and difficult journey to prison in Martin. They had several stops during their journey, during which Viera Čunderlíková took care of the wounded. When they arrived in Martin, Viera Čunderlíková was interrogated and sent to the concentration camp in Mathausen. She waited for transportation in the prison in Martin. She thought of escape more and more. From this moment she experienced several fortunate events.[40]

A certain warder suggested helping her escape. He used an opportunity when soldiers had got drunk. Seven more people managed to escape from the prison. However, she got into trouble after her escape. She did not have any cash or documents. There was a high risk that she would be arrested again, so she decided to go home. She went to the station where a stranger helped her again. It was a woman holding a little child. This woman gave Viera her luggage for unknown reasons. When she got on the train, the conductor found out she did not have a ticket, but he did not throw her off the train. From Martin she continued by train to Banská Bystrica which had filled up with the members of the Hlinka Guard and German units in the meantime. She got home thanks to a stroke of luck. A coachman gave her a ride home. He had permission from the German authorities which enabled him to pass individual patrols without any problems. She arrived home late at night and found that it was full of enemy soldiers who were sleeping at the time. Thanks to her grandmother she hid in a stove where she waited until morning. In the morning she went to the woods where she sought shelter and safety. She reached a partisan group led by Daniel Chladný.[41] There she took care of the wounded and sick and worked as

40 *Životopis Viery Malatovej.* Archive of the Ministry of Interior of SR – Military historical archive, *Profesionálne a sociálne skupiny v SNP*, file Živena, Burajová, *Životopisy žien – Účastníčok SNP,* 59.

41 Daniel Chladný led the fifth division of the partisan brigade called Smrť fašizmu (Death to Fascism) after the suppression of the Slovak National Uprising. He operated in the woods in the surroundings of Banská Bystrica. Source: Plevza, *Dejiny Slovenského,* 183.

a cook, too. Her life is fascinating due to the fact that her life was saved thanks to several happy coincidences and she managed to avoid the concentration camp in Mathausen. In this way she was able to provide those who needed it with medical care.[42]

Margita Máleková

She was born Margita Martinková on November 10, 1920 in Handlová. She took part in the Slovak National Uprising, in which she worked as a nurse, and she also took part in several battles with a gun in her hand. She received several awards for her activity in the Slovak National Uprising, such as the Order of the Slovak National Uprising of the third class as well as commemorative medals for the anniversaries of the Slovak National Uprising.[43]

She came from a family of five children. Her father, Ján Martinka, was a co-founder of the communist party in Handlová. Margita Martinková could not find a job for a long time. At first she earned her living as a laborer for bricklayers, which cannot be considered a typical activity for women even nowadays. However, it was already clear at that time that she did not mind hard work.[44]

Her life started to change when she got an offer from the then chief physician of the hospital in Handlová, MUDr. Rehák, who gave her the opportunity to do a nursing course. Margita accepted this offer and later used the knowledge from this course mainly during the Slovak National Uprising.[45]

---

42 *Životopis Viery Malatovej.* Archive of the Ministry of Interior of SR – Military historical archive, *Profesionálne a sociálne skupiny v SNP,* file Živena, Burajová, *Životopisy žien – Účastníčok SNP,* 59.

43 *Životopis Margity Málekovej.* Archive of the Ministry of Interior of SR – Military historical archive, *Profesionálne a sociálne skupiny v SNP,* file Živena, Mihálikova, *Životopisy žien – Účastníčok SNP,* 63.

44 *Životopis Margity Málekovej.* Archive of the Ministry of Interior of SR – Military historical archive, *Profesionálne a sociálne skupiny v SNP,* file Živena, Mihálikova, *Životopisy žien – Účastníčok SNP,* 63.

45 *Životopis Margity Málekovej.* Archive of the Ministry of Interior of SR – Military historical archive, *Profesionálne a sociálne skupiny v SNP,* file Živena, Mihálikova, *Životopisy žien – Účastníčok SNP,* 63.

Several events anticipated the armed conflict that would sooner or later come to Handlová. Explosives from military warehouses in Handlová started to disappear and 200 men had left the town before the Slovak National Uprising broke out. At the end of August 1944, it was said that partisan units were going to occupy the town. There were several people of German origin in Handlová. The local German minority[46] also started to prepare for an armed clash with partisan units.[47]

Not only Handlová, but also its surroundings were involved in the battles. The first wounded treated by Margita Martinková were from battlefields in the surroundings of Partizánske. These soldiers were transported to the hospital in Handlová, where Alexej Semionovič Jegorov worked as a commander during the Slovak National Uprising.[48]

Fighting in the surroundings of Handlová became more and more intense. German units started to gain the upper hand thanks to superior armaments. Partisan units were forced to retreat due to these circumstances. The evacuation of the hospital in Handlová took place at the same time. Patients were divided between hospitals in Zvolen, Svätý Kríž nad Hronom (today's Žiar nad Hronom) and Sliač. Several civilians joined the patients as well.[49]

The main partisan headquarters in Banská Bystrica became the new posting for Margita Martinková after the evacuation. Several days later, she moved to the first partisan brigade of M. R. Štefánik due to a lack of nurses. P. A. Veličko was the commander of this brigade. Margita was sent to the Suvorov division.[50] As her posting had changed from a hospital to

---

46 More about the issue of German population in Slovakia. Source: Horváthová, *Nemci na Slovensku: Etnokultúrne tradície z aspektu osídlenia, remesiel a odievania.* 2002.
47 *Životopis Margity Málekovej.* Archive of the Ministry of Interior of SR – Military historical archive, *Profesionálne a sociálne skupiny v SNP,* file Živena, Miháliková, *Životopisy žien – Účastníčok SNP,* 63.
48 *Životopis Margity Málekovej.* Archive of the Ministry of Interior of SR – Military historical archive, *Profesionálne a sociálne skupiny v SNP,* file Živena, Miháliková, *Životopisy žien – Účastníčok SNP,* 63.
49 *Životopis Margity Málekovej.* Archive of the Ministry of Interior of SR – Military historical archive, *Profesionálne a sociálne skupiny v SNP,* file Živena, Miháliková, *Životopisy žien – Účastníčok SNP,* 63.
50 Lacko, *Slovenské národné,* 67–68.

a military division, it was highly likely that she would experience battle. For this reason, she underwent training where she learnt how to shoot various types of weapon.[51]

She experienced her first battle in Svätý Kríž nad Hronom. Then she participated in battles at Tomášovce, Lovinobaňa and Cinobaňa. In the end, the Suvorov division moved to the surroundings of Vígľaš where they met the commander of the brigade of M. R. Štefánik, V. A. Veličko. The preceding battles with the participation of the Suvorov division took their toll in the form of casualties and utter exhaustion. They had a little time to rest there. However, this rest for the Suvorov division, and thus for Margita Martinková, did not last for long.[52]

There were increasing commands to retreat due to the fact that the partisan units were being pushed back. The Suvorov division also received a command to retreat just after they had arrived in the surroundings of Vígľaš. This division was supposed to retreat in the direction of Banská Bystrica. This happened in October 1944. The weather was cold and rainy. The terrain in the woods was difficult. Margita's bad health made her situation even more complicated. Her work took its toll in the form of rheumatism and later she also contracted typhus. She knew that she could not stay with the Suvorov division in such a condition. She would cause problems not only for herself, but also for the rest of the group. That is why she decided to leave the division and go to Zvolen.[53]

As has been already mentioned, a number of patients were evacuated from the hospital in Handlová to Zvolen. There were also some inhabitants from Handlová who decided to leave their hometown. Margita stayed in Zvolen for several days and then she went back to her family. She arrived in bad health and also found out that the Gestapo had visited her mother

51 *Životopis Margity Málekovej*. Archive of the Ministry of Interior of SR – Military historical archive, *Profesionálne a sociálne skupiny v SNP*, file Živena, Mihálikova, *Životopisy žien – Účastníčok SNP*, 63.

52 *Životopis Margity Málekovej*. Archive of the Ministry of Interior of SR – Military historical archive, *Profesionálne a sociálne skupiny v SNP*, file Živena, Mihálikova, *Životopisy žien – Účastníčok SNP*, 63.

53 *Životopis Margity Málekovej*. Archive of the Ministry of Interior of SR – Military historical archive, *Profesionálne a sociálne skupiny v SNP*, file Živena, Mihálikova, *Životopisy žien – Účastníčok SNP*, 63.

very often. The reason for these frequent and undesirable visits was simple – her father was a famous communist. Margita's mother was able to hide her but her health condition required urgent medical treatment. The former chief physician of the hospital in Handlová, the above-mentioned Dr. Rehák, thanks to whom she had become a nurse, took care of her.[54]

Her health condition improved after some time, but new complications set in on December 12, 1944 when all of her family was thrown out of their house. They eventually found shelter in a local bank. Margita was also transported to this building although she had not totally recovered. Margita Martinková learnt about the end of the war on April 4 in Handlová. Her brother and cousin did not survive the war. It is also worth mentioning that Rudolf Málek became her husband. He fought in the partisan brigade of M. R. Štefánik, but was a member of a different division. They met each other at a celebration held in honor of the partisans.[55]

Mária Mitická

Her maiden name was Mária Kováčová. She was born on May 27, 1922. Pezinok was her hometown. She took part in the Slovak National Uprising as a nurse in the Belov division[56] which was a part of the Jegorov partisan brigade. She was awarded the Badge of the Czechoslovak Partisan for her activities in the Slovak National Uprising and she is a holder of the Commemorative Medal for the 40th anniversary of the liberation.[57]

She came from a family of eight children. Her mother died when she was six. She started to work in paper production in Ružomberok at quite

54 *Životopis Margity Málekovej*. Archive of the Ministry of Interior of SR – Military historical archive, *Profesionálne a sociálne skupiny v SNP*, file Živena, Miháliková, *Životopisy žien – Účastníčok SNP*, 63.
55 *Životopis Margity Málekovej*. Archive of the Ministry of Interior of SR – Military historical archive, *Profesionálne a sociálne skupiny v SNP*, file Živena, Miháliková, *Životopisy žien – Účastníčok SNP*, 63.
56 *Životopis Márie Mitickej*. Archive of the Ministry of Interior of SR – Military historical archive, *Profesionálne a sociálne skupiny v SNP*, file Živena, Ťapajová, *Životopisy žien – Účastníčok SNP*, 75.
57 *Životopis Márie Mitickej*. Archive of the Ministry of Interior of SR – Military historical archive, *Profesionálne a sociálne skupiny v SNP*, file Živena, Ťapajová, *Životopisy žien – Účastníčok SNP*, 75.

an early age. When the Slovak National Uprising broke out, she did a voluntary nursing course. She was then assigned to the Belov division, which was part of the Jegorov partisan brigade. She took part in her first battles in the surroundings of Vrútky as early as September 1944. Mária Kováčová was injured during this fighting when she tried to treat the wounded in the middle of the battlefield. She was wounded in the head, shoulder and leg. Despite being hit several times, she survived and was transported to the hospital in Martin.[58]

When her condition had stabilized, she was moved from Martin to the hospital in Sliač and then to Kováčová for convalescence. After her recovery, she started to help partisans with activities such as cooking and washing clothes, and she still worked as a nurse, too. She also delivered messages in the surroundings of Banská Bystrica.[59]

Delivering messages was among the riskiest of tasks. She could be exposed and arrested or even killed. Mária Kováčová came under crossfire in the surroundings of Staré hory while she was fulfilling one of these missions. She tried to escape and managed it for a time. However, she was captured at Svätý kríž in the surroundings of Liptovský Mikuláš and interrogated by enemy units. She was suspected of being a partisan. During the interrogation, Mária claimed that she had been attacked by some unknown soldiers in the woods and that she had only been trying to get to safety. It is not clear whether the interrogators believed her or not.[60]

She managed to escape from this situation thanks to a stranger who wore a police uniform and was close to the interrogators. He helped her escape from custody and sent her to his sister in Kremnica where she hid for the night. Then she went back to her native Pezinok where started to

---

58 *Životopis Márie Mitickej*. Archive of the Ministry of Interior of SR – Military historical archive, *Profesionálne a sociálne skupiny v SNP*, file Živena, Ťapajová, *Životopisy žien – Účastníčok SNP*, 75.

59 *Životopis Márie Mitickej*. Archive of the Ministry of Interior of SR – Military historical archive, *Profesionálne a sociálne skupiny v SNP*, file Živena, Ťapajová, *Životopisy žien – Účastníčok SNP*, 75.

60 *Životopis Márie Mitickej*. Archive of the Ministry of Interior of SR – Military historical archive, *Profesionálne a sociálne skupiny v SNP*, file Živena, Ťapajová, *Životopisy žien – Účastníčok SNP*, 75.

work as an aid in a local hospital. She stayed in Pezinok until the end of war, i.e., until the arrival of the Red Army.[61]

Pplk. MUDr. Lívia Rizničová

She was born in Spišská Nová Ves as Lívia Bravdová on March 28, 1928. She was an active participant in the Slovak National Uprising. She worked in the division of Major Morozov and then in the division of A. S. Jegorov as a nurse. She received several awards such as For the Service to the Motherland, For the Defense of the Motherland and For the Participation in the Slovak National Uprising, and she was also given several commemorative medals for individual anniversaries of the Slovak National Uprising.[62]

When the Slovak National Uprising broke out, Lívia Bravdová was 16. She was a very interesting woman – she joined several men heading for Banská Bystrica to strengthen the uprising which had just started. When these men arrived in Banská Bystrica, they were assigned to individual military partisan divisions.[63]

However, there was a problem in assigning Lívia. At first she helped partisan units with various activities. Later she became a nurse. In October 1944, the situation of the rebels dramatically worsened. German units were arriving closer to the center of the uprising – Banská Bystrica. The headquarters gave partisans in this central Slovak town the command to retreat. Lívia also started to retreat.[64] Baláže, situated close to Banská Bystrica, was their retreat destination.[65]

---

61 *Životopis Márie Mitickej*. Archive of the Ministry of Interior of SR – Military historical archive, *Profesionálne a sociálne skupiny v SNP*, file Živena, Ťapajová, *Životopisy žien – Účastníčok SNP*, 75.

62 *Životopis Pplk. MUDr. Lívie Rizničovej*. Archive of the Ministry of Interior of SR – Military historical archive, *Profesionálne a sociálne skupiny v SNP*, file Živena, Drobová, *Životopisy žien – Účastníčok SNP*, 75.

63 *Životopis Pplk. MUDr. Lívie Rizničovej*. Archive of the Ministry of Interior of SR – Military historical archive, *Profesionálne a sociálne skupiny v SNP*, file Živena, Drobová, *Životopisy žien – Účastníčok SNP*, 75.

64 *Životopis Pplk. MUDr. Lívie Rizničovej*. Archív Ministerstva vnútra SR – Vojenský historický archív, fond *Profesionálne a sociálne skupiny v SNP*, zložka Živena, Drobová, *Životopisy žien – Účastníčok SNP*, 75.

65 Plevza, *Dejiny Slovenského*, 394.

The village of Baláže became the first real battlefield for Lívia. When the partisans arrived in this village, vicious fighting with German units started. It was a chaotic situation for Lívia, who had not participated in a real battle before. That is why she decided to hide in a nearby stall. She stayed there until the situation had calmed. Then she escaped to nearby bushes where she tried to hide from subsequent fighting. She met several partisans in the woods close to Baláže. She reached the partisan division of Major Morozov[66] together with them. She helped with various activities in this division.[67]

When Lívia Bravdová arrived to relative safety, another problem arose. The partisan group with whom Lívia stayed had started to run out of supplies. It was only possible to get them in the surrounding villages, but they were guarded by the enemy. That is why Lívia as a woman was in charge of this task. She was supposed to arouse less suspicion and sneak around the enemy patrols without being noticed and get food. However, she was discovered and arrested by an enemy patrol while fulfilling this task.[68]

Lívia was supposed to be taken to Kremnička. However, this transport was attacked by partisan units. Lívia used the crossfire and chaos to escape to nearby woods. The enemy started to search for her. While wandering around the woods in the surroundings of Baláže, she met Ondrej Ivanič Červeň, who had a farm on this territory. This man provided her with safe shelter for some time where she hid from the enemy patrols looking for her. They even searched for her at Ondrej Ivanič Červeň's farm and stayed in his hay barn for a night. However, Lívia was not discovered.[69]

---

66 Major Semion Georgijević Morozov – he led the partisan division Pomstiteľ (Avenger). Source: Plevza, *Dejiny Slovenského*, 408, 511.

67 *Životopis Pplk. MUDr. Lívie Rizničovej*. Archive of the Ministry of Interior of SR – Military historical archive, *Profesionálne a sociálne skupiny v SNP*, file Živena, Drobová, *Životopisy žien – Účastníčok SNP*, 75.

68 *Životopis Pplk. MUDr. Lívie Rizničovej*. Archive of the Ministry of Interior of SR – Military historical archive, *Profesionálne a sociálne skupiny v SNP*, file Živena, Drobová,*Životopisy žien – Účastníčok SNP*, 75.

69 *Životopis Pplk. MUDr. Lívie Rizničovej*. Archive of the Ministry of Interior of SR – Military historical archive, *Profesionálne a sociálne skupiny v SNP*, file Živena, Drobová, *Životopisy žien – Účastníčok SNP*, 75.

When they left, partisans from the Jegorov division came to Červeň. Lívia joined them without hesitation. She worked as a nurse in this division where she stayed until the end of the war and arrival of the Red Army. After the war, she started to study medicine in Hradec Králové.[70]

Zuzana Šinglerová

She was born on July 7, 1923 in Hnúšťa. Her maiden name was Zuzana Manicová. She served in the Slovak National Uprising as a nurse and scout. She was awarded the Order of the Slovak National Uprising of the third class, various commemorative medals for individual anniversaries of the Slovak National Uprising as well as the Award for Excellent Work.[71]

News of the beginning of World War II reached Zuzana in Prague where she worked as a servant. She was a witness to the arrival of the first German units which entered Prague in 1939. This fact as well as worries about her mother influenced her decision to go back to Slovakia, to Tisovec, where her mother had moved from Hnúšťa.[72]

When she arrived there, she found out that her brothers had been participating in Communist Party meetings, which had become illegal in the territory of Slovakia.[73] Fear of being revealed did not discourage her and she took part in one of these meetings. Karol Šmidke[74] was also present. He made a speech in which he appealed for seditious activities against the regime. He discussed informing people by means of the press, and

---

70 *Životopis Pplk. MUDr. Lívie Rizničovej.* Archive of the Ministry of Interior of SR – Military historical archive, *Profesionálne a sociálne skupiny v SNP,* file Živena, Drobová, *Životopisy žien – Účastníčok SNP,* 75.

71 *Životopis Zuzany Šinglerovej.* Archive of the Ministry of Interior of SR – Military historical archive, *Profesionálne a sociálne skupiny v SNP,* file Živena, Burajová, *Životopisy žien – Účastníčok SNP,* 119.

72 *Životopis Zuzany Šinglerovej.* Archive of the Ministry of Interior of SR – Military historical archive, *Profesionálne a sociálne skupiny v SNP,* file Živena, Burajová, *Životopisy žien – Účastníčok SNP,* 119.

73 Sokolovič, *Perzekúcie na Slovensku v rokoch 1938–1945,* 68, 77.

74 Karol Šimdke – he played a significant role in anti-fascist activities and he was also one of the cofounders of the illegal Slovak National Council. Rychlík, *Češi a Slováci ve 20.století: Česko-slovenské vztahy 1914–1945,* 269.

weapon gathering. During this meeting, Zuzana also met her future husband, Pavol Šingler, a local communist who had several sympathizers.[75]

The wedding of Zuzana Manicová and Pavol Šingler took place about six months before the beginning of the Slovak National Uprising. When it broke out, Zuzana and her husband with several other men went directly to the center of the event, to Banská Bystrica. When they arrived, Zuzana Šinglerová was assigned to a field hospital situated in Tri duby[76]. She took part in a nursing course there and helped with nursing activities at the same time. The patients of the field hospital at the airport of Tri duby were of different nationalities, so Zuzana treated not only Slovaks but also wounded French and Soviet soldiers.[77]

A command to evacuate the hospital came in October 1944 due to the retreat of the partisan units in this area. The wounded were transported to the school in Tisovec[78] which functioned as an emergency hospital. They started to run out of medical supplies very quickly, especially anesthetic. Diluted alcohol was used instead, but they soon started to run out of that as well. Zuzana Šinglerová managed to get a kind of cognac which was used as an anesthetic at least for some time.[79]

Another evacuation came soon after. The temporary hospital in Tisovec was evacuated again on October 21, 1944. The wounded were divided into two groups. Those with more serious injuries were transported by train to the approaching Red Army. Patients with minor injuries were placed and hidden in the surrounding houses. After the patients from Tisovec had

---

75 *Životopis Zuzany Šinglerovej*. Archive of the Ministry of Interior of SR – Military historical archive, *Profesionálne a sociálne skupiny v SNP*, file Živena, Burajová, *Životopisy žien – Účastníčok SNP*, 119.

76 The airport Tri duby was also situated in this place. It was the most significant airport during the Slovak National Uprising. Source: Jablonický, *Povstanie bez legiend: dvadsať kapitol o príprave a začiatku Slovenského národného povstania*, 309.

77 *Životopis Zuzany Šinglerovej*. Archive of the Ministry of Interior of SR – Military historical archive, *Profesionálne a sociálne skupiny v SNP*, file Živena, Burajová, *Životopisy žien – Účastníčok SNP*, 119.

78 Plevza, *Dejiny Slovenského*, 407.

79 *Životopis Zuzany Šinglerovej*. Archive of the Ministry of Interior of SR – Military historical archive, *Profesionálne a sociálne skupiny v SNP*, file Živena, Burajová, *Životopisy žien – Účastníčok SNP*, 119.

been evacuated, Zuzana and her mother hid in the surrounding woods where they met several partisans. These men were in bad condition caused not only by the cold and damp weather but also by a lack of basic supplies. Zuzana Šinglerová risked being arrested and went to Tisovec to provide these men at least with basic supplies such as food and warm clothes. However, Tisovec had already fallen under enemy control. News of the end of the war reached her in the woods in the surroundings of Tisovec in the company of the partisans.[80]

---

80 *Životopis Zuzany Šinglerovej.* Archive of the Ministry of Interior of SR – Military historical archive, *Profesionálne a sociálne skupiny v SNP*, file Živena, Burajová, *Životopisy žien – Účastníčok SNP*, 119.

Judita Szekeresová Kovácsová

Significant figures of the municipality of Pered during the interwar period

Abstract: This chapter shows a view of some of the most significant figures of the municipality of Pered during the interwar period. Through the lifes of these people we can recognize the changes that happened in this period. First the end of Word War I, the disintegration of the Austro- Hungarian monarchy and the birth of Czechoslovakia. They were not only inhabitants of the village, but influential members of the local society, and helped to weave its social and economic fabric. This chapter aims to show more than just the typical life of a teacher, a miller, doctor, but also what is beyond.The main sources are archival documents from official and private legacy, which are expanded with the secondary informations from the Slovak and Hungarian expert literature.

Keywords: Pered, teacher, doctor, miller, grocer, rector, pharmacist, fireman, interwar period

Wars change lives and affect the very foundations of the legacy that our ancestors have built for us. Life during periods of conflict is often extremely hard. People who have worked to overcome this adversity and accomplish something beneficial for their communities during times of war (and, of course, in its aftermath) were often fascinating members of communal life. They tried to use their energy, intelligence and experience to build a better life for all. The village of Pered (now named Tešedíkovo after the famous teacher Samuel Tešedik[1]) is situated in the southwest of Slovakia, in the Danubian Lowland. The fertility of the soil in this area led to a historical reliance on agriculture.[2] The village is first mentioned in the historical

---

1 The village of Tešedíkovo used the name of Pered until 1948. In February, it changed it to Tešedíkovo. It was named after Samuel Tešedík. He was an Evangelical priest, teacher and folk farmer. He worked in Szarvas (the village Sarvaš is currently situated in Hungary). Tešedíkovo is one of the 13 villages which did not get back their original names after 1990.

2 Tešedíkovo (Hungarian: Pered) is a village and municipality in the Šaľa District, Nitra Region, in the southwest of Slovakia. It covers an area of 2,278 ha and

record in 1237. After the Austro-Hungarian army had disintegrated in November 1918, Czechoslovak troops occupied the area – an occupation later recognized internationally by the Treaty of Trianon.

This article introduces some of the noted individuals who lived in Pered between the world wars (WWI and WWII). They were not only inhabitants of the village, but influential members, and helped weave its social and economic fabric. They were not mere teachers, millers, firemen and so on. They were an intrinsic part of the life of the village and did something extraordinary for their community: they became part of its history.

Teachers

The profession of teacher is an ancient, life-long and demanding vocation. Not only is adequate training important for teaching, but teachers need a great deal of courage and patience, and a lot of humor. Most important is a love for children, for education and for knowledge. A teacher is a person who is only happy when sharing wisdom and knowledge with someone else, and passing it on to generation after generation.

Throughout history, the teacher was a learned and recognized person in the community. He was remembered everywhere that he taught. Historically speaking, the teacher was maybe the only person (besides the priest) who was able to read and write. Teachers played very important roles in education and cultural associations. They helped children not only in their education, but sometimes acted as role-models for them.

---

is regarded as a medium-large village in Slovakia. The terrain is slightly flat with little forest. There are not enough minerals in the soil, but the temperate climate is good for agriculture. The village is surrounded by waterways – to the north, the River Váh and to the west, the MalýDunaj (Little Danube) and its tributaries. Tešedíkovo has many neighboring villages: Diakovce, Šaľa, Hetmín, Žihárec, Kráľov Brod and Dolné Saliby. The closest cities are Galanta, Nové Zámky, Kolárovo, Komárno and to the west, Dunajská Streda.

József Hüttner
"The friendly teacher"

A well-known teacher in Pered, between the wars, was József Hüttner. He was the long-time head teacher at the Roman Catholic elementary school.

József Hüttner was born on February 20, 1886 to the family of Márton Hüttner and Borbála Sviker in Duanakiliti (now situated in Hungary). He attended the elementary school during 1892–1898 in Rohovce; in 1898, he started to attend the local school in Šamorín, where he finished his studies in 1902. That year, he started to study at the Teacher's Academy in Modra, where he graduated as a teacher in 1906.[3]This was a happy time for him because in this year, he started to teach in Pered.[4] We do not know exactly when he moved to Pered, and no person in his family does either. We suppose only that it was maybe after he started teaching there. He was chosen as a teacher during a session of the Roman Catholic See on November 11, 1906. He had two challengers: Július Lengyel and Ľudovít Vogh. In the minutes, it is written that he was chosen unanimously. He not only found employment, but he was also given teacher's accommodation. It was one room with heating and cleaning. He lived in the cantor's house. His duties included not only teaching, but he had to escort children to the church and back to school. It was a Catholic school and he had to attend many different Catholic processions where he had to take care of his pupils. His responsibilities included paying taxes and every teacher had to teach in the repeating class. After his nomination, he swore that he would act according to his conscience and responsibilities.[5]

In 1907, a new school was built in Pered; this building was extended with three new teachers' apartments. This event proved serendipitous for József. During the 1912–1913 term, the school prepared these three flats

---

3   Slovak National Archive in Bratislava, hereinafter SNA BA. Fond (hereinafter f.) Commission of Education hereinafter f. PoŠk. 42695/1933, box n. 1217
4   Chronicle of the Hungarian Language Elementary School in Tešedíkovo (1925–1941). Jozef Darázss's transcription.
5   State Archive in Nitra, Šaľa department, hereinafter SANR SA. f. Parochial Office in Tešedíkovo, hereinafter FÚ Tešedíkovo. School Board Memorandum 1931–1947, box n. 6.

and three new teachers were employed. Among these teachers, there was his future wife, Emerencia Szilvássi from Topoľnica.[6]

During WWI, teachers had to participate in battle. The war was an event that affected everybody's lives very deeply – students, their families and teachers too. József Hüttner was in actual military service as a lieutenant during the summer holiday in 1908. Military service as an infantry lieutenant during WWI lasted from August 1914 to December 1918. We can say that he fought the whole of WWI.[7] His granddaughter reflects in her recollections that he fought on the Italian front, where he was shot in the knee. From this time onwards, he suffered pain in his knee.[8] But it can be said that he was lucky, because his colleague, Béla Csáp, did not only suffer injury, but died during WWI. József returned after his war experiences, full of enthusiasm to teach his pupils.

In 1922, he had full autonomy in his teaching. He usually taught classes I and II. During his teaching he tried to deliver his pupils new knowledge scrupulously and conscientiously. He not only touched on temporary subjects, he prepared his pupils for different celebration performances, for example, Christmas celebrations, celebrations of the formation of the Czechoslovak Republic, Mother's Day, different church celebrations and so on.

József Hüttner's family spoke his mother tongue, Hungarian. In his personal file, it is written that he could speak Slovak with minor mistakes. He tried to improve in this language as well as in grammar. In August 1922, he and his wife passed the homologation exam in accordance with law No 276 of 1920. This exam allowed them to practice their profession in Slovak.

---

6   Emerencia Szilvási was born on December 6, 1887 in Topoľnica. She attended elementary school in her home village; during 1898–1902, she studied at a local school in Bratislava and she studied at the Institute for Teachers in Bratislava too. She graduated in 1906. First, she worked at the Elementary School in Trstice, later at the Roman Catholic School in Pered. She retired in May 1947. She and her husband worked all their lives at the school; they loved children and pedagogy.

7   SNA BA. f. PoŠk. 42695/1933, box n. 1217.

8   Beáta Kopáčiková, Malinovo, email message to author, September 28, 2015.

The "Little law" in 1922 brought lots of changes in education in all of the Czechoslovak Republic. This law was No 226/1922, and changed all national school systems. It meant that obligatory attendance was eight years, and along with public schools, kindergartens were established. They belonged to the state and were responsible of taking care of children from the age of 3 to 6. Public schools used to be church schools, but they could be state and private.[9]

József Hüttner married Emerencia Szilvássi on June 25, 1922. Their daughter Helena Izabella was born in May 1927. They also had an adoptive daughter. It is not known when they adopted Gizela Szilvássi. She was the daughter of Emerencia's brother.[10] He lived in very poor circumstances in the territory of present-day Hungary. The Hüttners were trying to help the Szilvássi family. This pays testimony to Hüttner's love of children and his respect for his family. She was treated by them as their own daughter. They helped her very much; she studied as other children in normal families. She passed her Maturita exams. For Izabella she was like a sister; she did not have her own siblings. They were contemporaries, which made it easier for them to become best friends.[11]

The Hüttner family had their own family house in Tešedíkovo, built by Jozef Hüttner. Nowadays you can still see this house in Tešedíkovo. The owners are not members of the Hüttner family but most parts of the house are still in their original condition. For that time, it was a very modern house. In this house, they had one section with three rooms and a cellar. Their granddaughter recalls that her grandparents had their own servant and she helped them with the housework. The family had another servant who helped with taking care of their daughters.

---

9   This school law was accepted by the National Assembly on July 13, 1922. It was called the "little law" because it governed the school system only partly. This school system was accepted before the First Czechoslovak Republic was established. It introduced new school subjects into the system of education such as civics, handicrafts and so on. It stated that female and male teachers were equal. Kováč, *Kronika Slovenska 2. Slovensko v dvadsiatom storočí*, 129.

10 SNA BA. f. PoŠk. 42695/1933, box n. 1217.

11 Gizela worked all her life at the Post Office. She had one brother who stayed with their parents; he worked as a farmer. Beáta Kopáčiková, Malinovo, email message to author, September 28, 2015..

In the academic year 1929–1930, Alojz Horváth, the head teacher of the school in Pered, wanted to retire. József Hüttner was elected as the head teacher in August 1930. In the academic year 1930–1931, 710 schoolchildren attended the school. There were ten classes in the school, but there were, for example, two classes in the first grade. The school did not have enough space for teaching, so it implemented a plan: there were two classes in grade I, Class I and Class I.A. They divided the teaching: girls attended school in the morning and boys in the afternoon. József Hüttner had both of them under his care.[12] The following year he was the class teacher for Class II. As the head teacher, he received a lot of administrative work and as a teacher, he was a class teacher. His wife was the class teacher of Class I, but she taught handicrafts to older students.

Teachers are usually eternal students. József Hüttner is an example of this. He completed a course in drawing in 1929 in Galanta.[13]

The year 1931 brought a lot of changes to the school in Pered. On May 10 of this year, the parent-teacher association was founded. It had 40 members; the lay chairman was József Hüttner.

On October 25, 1931, students of the Roman Catholic school in Pered participated in a celebration where a memorial of soldiers who died in WWI was held. Students had a performance. They had a large audience from the village as well as from neighboring villages.[14]

Hüttner's wife was a very active person too. In 1932, she tried to found folk courses. She was elected to the local committee for education. Their main task was to found folk courses for women. These courses were for adult women and teaching was in the afternoon or evening in the school building.

Hüttner was very honest, loved teaching and tried to help everybody. Evidence of this is that he helped at a charity event for poor children in the school in 1934. In their name, he wrote a request for help in the form of a student's book. This letter together with the children's signatures was sent

---

12 Chronicle of the Hungarian elementary school in Tešedíkovo (1925–1941). Jozef Darázss's transcription.
13 SNA BA.f.PoŠk. 42695/1933, box n. 1217.
14 Chronicle of Hungarian elementary school in Tešedíkovo (1925–1941). Jozef Darázss's transcription.

to the District Office in Šaľa. The office helped the students.[15] They were extremely pleased. József Hüttner together with his students wrote a thank you letter to the District Office in Šaľa for their help.[16]

After the Vienna Award in 1938, the village of Pered became part of Hungary. WWII came as a great shock to the Hüttners. Their house was occupied by Soviet officers. Hüttner with his family had to live in one room. During the war he did not have a salary and their life was very hard because his wife was only a teacher. They did not have their own animals and garden.

Despite a lot of changes in the political situation, in the village he still remained in his profession, as a teacher and in his function of head. In 1939, he was elected as a notary on the representative council of the Roman Catholic community. In this session he was elected as the chairman of the Department of Faith and Deportment in Pered.[17]

As a teacher, he had many tasks not only involving the teaching and raising of children, but also preparing his pupils for countless performances, celebrations etc. He was very literate and bought newspapers and magazines. He had a radio and it was the reason that he knew about much of the news in the world.

In 1940, after 34 years of teaching at the school in Pered, the Roman Catholic school council decided to promote him, so he was promoted to 3rd degree and to 7th salary class. In the minutes, it was written that he did his work very conscientiously.[18] He was forced to do his 14-day-long military service in Vozokany, Komárno and Győr in present-day Hungary during WWII.

Pered was awarded to Czechoslovakia after the war. József Hüttner was still the head of the school; in December 1945, he retired. However, he still served an extra year as a temporary teacher in the state school (it was the same school, but later it changed into a state school). He started his retirement in 1946.[19]

---

15 SANR SA. f. District in Šaľa (1922–1938), hereinafter f. OÚ SA. 13396/1934, box n. 382.
16 SANR SA. f. OÚ SA. 2076/1935, box n. 419.
17 SANR SA. f. FÚ Tešedíkovo. School Board Memorandum 1931–1947, box n. 6.
18 SANR SA. f. FÚ Tešedíkovo. József Hüttner's promotion, box n. 21.
19 SNA BA. f. PoŠk. 42695/1933, box n. 1217.

József Hüttner had a very democratic mentality; his views on life were direct and ethical – he never failed to live up to them. During the occupation of the southern part of present-day Slovakia, he was very respectful toward the history of Hungary and the history of the school. He tried to protect documents before their destruction and he hid lots of documents, maps and school pledges in his own house. He was very bold in this way.[20]

He served on the school council for many years after his retirement, and he was very dedicated to this role.

His daughter Izabella followed her parents; she studied at the University of Commenius in Bratislava and taught at the Pedagogical School in Bratislava and the gymnasium on Dunajská Street in Bratislava.

József Hüttner lived as a teacher all his life; he tried to live courageously, honestly and conscientiously. His work was about giving knowledge to pupils.

He passed away in 1968. He was very ill after developing pneumonia. He was buried in Pered. However, nobody from his family lives in this village. Beata, his granddaughter, still visits his grave and looks after it. It has recently been renovated.[21]

István Varga

"Cantor-teacher" or "Mr. Master"

István Varga was born on December 8, 1888 in Pered; his parents were Lipót Varga and Rozália Balázs. He grew up together with his sister Mária (her husband was the son of the local pub owner) and his brother József who stayed to work on the home farm. He attended elementary school during 1894–1910 in Pered, and then attended schools in Nové Zámky and Svätý Jur. In Esztergom on June 27, 1908, he graduated as a teacher. In this time his role was very important because a cantor-teacher was an important figure in the Catholic Church and Catholic schools.[22]

István Varga on October 2, 1908 got a job in Veľké Úľanyas a permanent teacher. He taught there only for two years. But via this job he met

---

20 SNA BA.f. PoŠk. 42695/1933, box n. 1217.
21 Beáta Kopáčiková, Malinovo, email message to author, September 28, 2015.
22 SNA BA. f. PoŠk. 56003/1933.

his wife, who came from there. Mária Pauer was a daughter of a local shop owner. Together they had three sons: László, Endre and Imre.

He raised his children very conscientiously. He tried to give them the best possible education, and taught them to love their birth places. However, each of his sons moved abroad. László and Imre lived in Budapest. Endre died during the war in the town of Focsani[23] in Romania. László was married in Budapest and worked as a manager in a company producing cables. He was in a high position because he could speak three languages (Slovak, Czech and Hungarian). He worked as a translator for the company. He traveled widely. He died in 2007, but his love for his own birth place was very strong. He wanted to be buried in Pered. His wife Margit transferred his ashes to the grave of his parents in the cemetery in Pered. Imre was a very famous graphic designer in Budapest. He was gifted and during family get-togethers he drew all of his family. His paintings and drawings were of a good standard and could be used to replace original photos.

In December 1910, he started his job in Horné Saliby where he taught at the Roman Catholic school until 1922. After this he was the head of the Roman Catholic school in Gabčíkovo; he remained there until the 1929–1930 academic year.[24]

Alajos Horváth, the school head in Pered retired after 43 years of teaching at this school.

He was not only a head, but a cantor-teacher too. The school board immediately decided to give him this job. He started to teach in September in 1930. On April 5, 1930, he made his religious vows together with his colleagues who were new teachers at the school. The vow was made in front of Ferenc Janics, who was the diocesan supervisor. István used to teach classes I and II.[25]

His work was interrupted by military service. In 1910, he was in full military service as a corporal in the 72nd regiment. Mobilization called teachers to duty too. István was enlisted in August 1914. During the war he was captured in Italy. He was there from September 1916 to April

---

23 Focşani is the capital of Vrancea County in Romania on the banks of the Milcov river, in the historical region of Moldavia.
24 SNA BA. f. PoŠk. 56003/1933.
25 SNA BA. f. PoŠk. 56003/1933.

1918.[26] He was a very able teacher although very strict. Sometimes he used his cane to punish his pupils. He got the nickname "nádpálcás" which means "the man with a cane". But with his strict teaching he achieved very good results. His love of music was very strong. His pupils loved his playing of the violin. One of his pupils remembers that when the teacher started playing on his violin the pupils forgot his punishments.[27]

After his return to the village he probably lived with his parents. Then later, a teacher's apartment was given to him which was near the school. He worked very hard as a cantor, but his relationships with rectors were not the best. In 1952, his wife passed away. His sons did not live in the village. He moved to a house where nuns lived. He died in 1970. His grave is in the cemetery in Pered.[28]

Members of the local economy

Pered, between the two wars, was an agricultural village, which meant that people had their own small farms and worked in agriculture. It was typical for this region, because there was a very conducive climate for agriculture. People also found jobs in local private businesses; the largest employer of villagers was the local mill. The first owner was Henrik Mészáros; then the business was led by his son-in-law, Cyprián Lelovics. It was a feature of Pered that in the village there were many pubs; people from Pered say that usually each 1–3 streets had their own pub. It was typical for young men to visit only their own local pub. Shop owners were usually Jewish. They often inherited these shops from their ancestors, who historically had been denied the opportunity to own land.

---

26 SNA BA. f. PoŠk. 56003/1933.
27 Gyula Varga, Tešedíkovo. According to a conversation with the author, October 26, 2016.
28 Gyula Varga, Tešedíkovo. According to a conversation with the author, October 26, 2016.

Henrik Mészáros

"The miraculous doctor"

Henrik Mészáros was the first owner of the mill in Pered. He was born in Pered on July 21, 1859. His parents were Ferenc Mészáros and Veronika Ürge. His mother came from the neighboring village of Žihárec. Firstly, he learned to be a shoemaker, but during his military service he tried to treat the sick. He had been a hussar in Oradea (Romania). It was a very important period in his life for him, because there he met his wife Zsófia László. During this marriage they had many children. First, his son Endre was born (December 19, 1884); then they had four daughters, Ilona (December 12, 1888), Erzsébet (March 30, 1892), Zsófia (June 14, 1898) and Anna (July 18, 1909).[29]

Endre – after his studies at the gymnasiums in Szarvas, Békescsaba and Trnava – went to study medicine in Munich. He became a doctor and displayed the talent and potential to be an able doctor, having inherited the skills to treat and diagnose from his father. After his studies, he married Paula Kern; she came from Vienna. Endre Mészáros died very young, probably of poisoning in 1911.[30]

Ilona, Henrik's daughter, was married in Csorvás in 1905. Her husband was Rajmund Naxner. They moved to Mödlingen in Austria. They had two sons, Rajmund and Henrik, there. Her husband died very soon in 1914, during a WWI battle on the Italian front. After his death Ilona moved away to America, where she married again. Her second husband was Károly Fülöp. During her life she traveled widely, although she spent most of her time in Budapest. At the end of her life, she was in Györgyszentiványi, where she died in 1969. She lived her last years with her partner, Florián Földváry. He died earlier than her and she lived together with his daughter.

Erzsébet became a nun in Temesvári in 1911. She was a Catholic nun in Temesvár, Lugos, Kolozsvár, Szeged, Battonya, Kiskunmajsa, Újszeged,

---

29 Three of their daughters (Mária, Veronika and Éva) and sons (István, Ferenc and Ádám) died in early childhood. Ádám was Éva's twin. SANR SA. Personal fund of the Meszáros-Lelovics family.

30 SANR SA. Personal fund of the Meszáros-Lelovics family. (Osobný fond rodinyMészáros – Lelovics).

Ludány and Budapest. From 1971, she was a nun in Jászberény, where she died in1982. She was buried in the nun's cemetery in Jászberény as Erzsébet-Aléna.

Henrik's youngest daughter, Anna, was married to her brother-in-law's brother, Ignác Lelovics. During this marriage three children were born: Mária, Ernő and Olivér. They lived near the mill. Ignác was a greaser at the mill. During the great fire, they were the most prominent helpers. They were buried in a common grave with Henrik Mészáros and his first wife.[31]

In Csorvás in 1870, there was a cholera outbreak; it was the reason why they built a hospital there. In this hospital, Henrik tried, as a 20-year-old man, to treat people. He was a self-taught medic.[32]

Several members of his family, especially members from his mother's side, had the ability to treat people. His uncle from his mother's side, Ignác Ürge, worked in China as a doctor; many hospitals in China were built by him.[33]Many contemporary magazines and newspapers wrote about his special abilities. He collected his knowledge during his military service in Arad. His special ability was in accurately diagnosing illnesses from the patients' hand and nail condition. He treated not only ordinary people, but more and more influential people were seeking his help. For example, a baroness from Csorvás was his patient. Many doctors from Csorvás and the surrounding area had tried to treat her illness, but only Henrik could help her. She was extremely grateful. She built a house for him and his family at 10 Kolcsey Street. A lot of people were jealous of him in Csorvás. More and more doctors and ordinary people were displeased by his treatments. They accused him of quackery. The most serious accusation was in 1905, and led to a fine of 400 crowns. He was not the only one subject to this accusation. His friend, Jenő Aczél, together with his assistant, György Kátai, who was a shoemaker too, were accused too. Many accusations stemmed from professional jealousy on the part of

31 Juraj Lelovics, Šaľa. According to a conversation with the author, October 1, 2016.
32 István Kasuba. *Csorvási Arcok 15. Mészáros Henrik. Csorvási Hírádó,* September 4, 1999.
33 One of his nephews, Ferenc (son of his brother Antal), worked in Neded and then in Csanádalbert, as a doctor.

other doctors and healers. Their principal problem was that when they were unable to successfully treat a patient, Henrik always knew how to help them. For example, in a particular case, Dr. Reisz accused Henrik after he had failed to treat József Fazekas who lived near Csorvás. Reisz's only recommendation had been to amputate Fazekas's leg. But Henrik knew how to help him.[34]

Although the accusations decreased, Henrik didn't stay in Csorvás. He donated his house to the Roman Catholic church in Csorvás. After 25 years of working in this place he went back to his home village of Pered. He bought the village mill. He was very successful because the mill was very prosperous and there the best flour of the region was made. Despite his entry into business, he never gave up his vocation. On average, he had 100 visitors who needed his help. According to a person from the village, it was said that sometimes ill people from very distant places came to see him and the queue in front of his house stretched to the end of his street. Ill people hoped that they would be cured. And often their faith in Henrik paid off.[35]

In his garden, he grew many herbs which he needed for his treatments. He knew what was effective for different illnesses. Sometimes he used not only plants, but insects too.

In 1926, his first wife László Zsófia died; she had been the mother of their children. On February 15, 1927, he married for the second time and his wife was a woman from Diakovce, Berta Nagy.[36] It isn't known why he married for a second time at his great age. There isn't much information about his second wife. The only information we have is that she was from Diakovce. Henrik's descendants said that his second wife had married him only for his money. In their memoirs, it is written that after his death she turned her back on their family and maybe on Pered too.

In the memoirs of his grandson Endre, we can read that he had a cellar in the back part of the house where all his patients came. There he sat often, reading and singing psalms. It was his dream to create a mud bath around

---

34 Documents from own family collection. Many effusive letters written for Henrik by his content patients.
35 SANR SA. Personal fund of Meszáros-Lelovics family.
36 SANRSA. f. OÚ SA,17598/1929, box n.192.

Lake Telektó. He loved horses and owned some. Perhaps this love for them came from his military service in Arad. There he performed his first operations on horses. He passed away after a short illness on November 9, 1932. He was suffering from tuberculosis and was 73 years old. His grave is in the cemetery in Pered near to that of his first wife.[37]

Cyprian Lelovics

"The miller with the title"

He was born on April 13, 1896 in Pered. His parents were Ferenc Lelovics and Katalin Mészáros. His family belonged to one that had received the title of yeoman in 1687.[38] His family had a coat of arms.[39] He had six siblings; one of his brothers, Ignác, married his sister-in-law, Anna Mészáros. His brother, Rafael, was the village reeve.

After attending Roman Catholic school from which he graduated in Pered, he started studying in Trnava. He became a butcher. He did this job until he became a miller. In the contemporary records, it is written that he was the owner of a salami producer during 1915–1920. This probably refers to his butcher's shop, which was in the mill in Pered.[40]

On June 22, 1915, he married Zsófia Mészáros, who was the daughter of Henrik Mészáros, the mill owner in Pered.[41] They had eight children. They were very well educated. The girls married into good families. His daughter Erzsébet (January 17, 1927) became the wife of a banker from

---

37 SANR SA. Personal fund of Meszáros-Lelovics family.

38 The family title given in 1687 was granted to György Lelovics and his wife Margit Hidegh. In this way their sons János and György received the title too. His brother, András Lelovics, and his wife, Ilona Aczél, and their descendants also received the title. Cyprian Lelovics was András Lelovics's desendant.

39 Sky blue military shield with green grass on three hills; on both sides are placed two stacks of wheat, in the middle an ostrich is standing straight and in its beak it is holding a ploughshare and turning to the right side of the shield. Above the shield there is a royal decorated military open helmet and above that are all the people's rams in red clothes, holding a decorative axe. At the back of the helmet decorative ornaments are hanging in glistening and red colors; they gradually fade and are beautiful and softly decorated.

40 Szeghalmy, Gyula. *Felvidék*, 231.

41 SANR SA. Personal fund of Meszáros-Lelovics family. Family photo album.

Šaľa (Zoltán Hanusz); Zsófia (May 21, 1919) married MUDr. Zoltán Feldmár, he was a long-time general practitioner in Pered; Katalin (May 11, 1922) married a soldier of the Hungarian Royal Army Aladár Török; later he became the head of the bank in Pered. Their son György (December 2, 1931) studied in Pardubice (now in the Czech Republic), and after his studies at the gymnasium in Komárno, he wanted to become a miller. However, after nationalization, he started to work as a driver, an occupation in which he worked for a long time. After a request by an agricultural company in Šaľa, he became head of the department of compound feed. There he worked until his retirement. His son Endre (August 18, 1920) became a rector, living in Zlaté Klasy for a long time; Cyprián (December 14, 1917) studied medicine. First, he worked as an army doctor, then a village doctor in Diakovce. Attila (June 23, 1930) started to work for Slovak Radio after his studies at gymnázium, first as an engineer and later as the main engineer. He died early in 1978. The youngest son, Tihamér (August 19, 1933), started to study pedagogy after his studies at the agricultural school. Then he taught at the elementary school in Trstice until his retirement.

Cyprián Lelovics left his job as a butcher and started to work first as a miller and later became the owner of the mill. He became owner after the death of his father-in-law, Henrik Mészáros in 1932. In this year, he obtained a trade license for trading as a miller.[42]It was probably during this time that he left his career as a butcher and started to work only as a miller. His knowledge of agriculture helped him obtain a gold charter for it. During his work there, the mill in Pered was one of the best mills in the district of Šaľa.

He belonged to the local intelligentsia, became involved in volunteering and loved hunting. He was a founding member of the Association of Volunteer Firemen in the village. The main reason was that the houses had thatched roofs and it was common for them to catch fire. Among the first members were villagers; later Cyprián joined together with Earl Ajtics Horváth Lóránt from Veča. They renewed the Association of Volunteer

---

42 SANR SA. (Main Service Office in Šaľa) Hlavnoslúžnovskýúrad Šaľa. Milling trade. 4087/1931, box n. 19.

Firemen because it had existed since 1885, but later it disappeared.[43] Many members of the future association wanted to have their own firemen in their village, and the association was revived in 1924.[44] Cyprián Lelovics became the Chairman of the Association of Volunteer Firemen in Pered; he was the head of the association until his death. In 1927, the firehouse was built and in this year, there was a consecration pledge of the association. His wife, Zsófia became the mother of the pledge.

Besides this, he was a member of many associations. He was a member of the school board. He was a chairman of the local consumer cooperative, local milk cooperative and was the deputy chairman of the Roman Catholic community board in Pered.

His membership of the local association of disabled was very important. It organized collecting of chamomile, lavender and paper and iron together. From the proceeds, they organized many social events for the members of this club.

After the nationalization of the mill, he started to work in a slaughterhouse in Nitra; there he worked until his formal retirement. Then he started to work at the Slovak National Savings Bank. A branch of this bank was established at his house; after that the husband of his daughter Elizabeth came into the family. He was a very amiable person. The bank

---

43 Many associations were suspended after WWI and then following the Austro-Hungarian Monarchy breaking up brought some changes. Associations established during The First Czechoslovak Republic were established in accordance with Law no. 1508, from November 15, 1875, which dealt with associations. Associations which had charters approved by the Hungarian Ministry of Home Affairs had to continue them (https://is.muni.cz/th/341838/ff_b/final.txt). A declaration on Firemen's Associations in 1921 created a new boom in them. It was the year that even a supra-provincial organization was established. The Ministry Plenipotentiary of Slovakia published on August 23, 1921, a regulation for all counties. It said it was obligatory for the organizations and protection services to establish fire departments. At the supra-provincial congress of fire departments in 1922, a "Yeoman" fire unit was established which had its seat in Turčiansky sv. Martin.

This fire unit oversaw all volunteer fire associations in Slovakia. Later district associations were established and their task was to establish village associations and help them in their work.

44 SANR SA, F. OÚ SA. Evidence of volunteer firemen associations.

opened only on Mondays and Thursdays, but he opened it many times out of opening hours. Many witnesses remember that he opened on several occasions when people required it. For example were someone died, he opened at midnight because people needed it. He was very helpful and had good relationships with the villagers. He could make people believe in opening a passbook and helped them to save their money for the future. He helped them to start building new houses and to choose loans.[45] In this time a new street (named "New Yard" – újtelep) was opened. A row of new houses for young families emerged there. He agitated for the sale of cinderblocks due to the shortage of building materials during the 1950–1970s. It was his way of helping the villagers.

In 1975, he with his wife celebrated their diamond wedding anniversary. There was a large celebration in the village hall and cultural center. They renewed their vows. At this celebration were their eight children, 22 grandchildren and 17 great grandchildren.[46]

He was one of the most important members of the village during the interwar period. Now his name is still mentioned in a positive light. He was a person who helped the village not only in an economic sense but he also helped to make a better community too. In the recollections of older villagers he was a very decent person, helpful and had a very open personality. He died on November 11, 1976. His grave is in the cemetery of Pered together with those of members of his family.

Jakab Goldstein

"Lébus – the best grocer in the village"

Jakab Goldstein was born on July 27, 1905 in Pered.[47] He was the only child of Leopold (Yehuda Areyeh) and his second wife, Magdalena (Lea, Léni) Blau. His nickname was Lajos Bácsi, which meant Uncle Ludwig. At birth he was named Jakab, but his aunt did not like the name and began

---

45 Juraj Lelovics, Šaľa. According to a conversation with author on October 1, 2016.
46 Chronicle of the village Pered No. 2 (1975–1978).
47 SANR SA. Notary Office in Pered, hereinafter f. NÚ Pered. Register of births, 1905.

calling him Ludwig, and the name stuck. Even in some official documents he was referred to as Ludwig. His father Leopold owned a grocery store in Pered. He completed his elementary studies and grammar school studies at the Jewish elementary school in Pered.[48] Then he learned business alongside his father. His father was a very able trader in the village. Jakab was an apprentice in his father's shop for three years, and then two years as an assistant.[49]After his father's death, his wife, Jakab's mother, became responsible for the business. Jakab and his mother succeeded. He ended his studies on February 6, 1935, and got his indenture.[50] He obtained his trade license on December 1, 1936; he was permitted to own a shop selling mixed goods.[51]

Jakab's education in business helped him greatly. He knew how to purchase huge quantities of merchandise and sell it for less than other stores in the village. He gained a good reputation and became known for his excellent service, cheap prices and readiness to serve the public.

He actually became a legend in the village. His mother used to call her husband in Yiddish, *Leb (it is the equivalent of the Hebrew Areyeh – Lion)*. Non-Jews heard it as "Lebush," (Lébus) and the nickname stuck for three generations. In the village there were always discussions about him and his grocery store, that "in Lebush's shop you can buy everything, only brain is not for sale in this shop". His father Leopold had numerous children with his first wife. She and two of the children died on the same night during an epidemic. Being considerably younger than the other children, he grew up without his siblings at home.

Jakab had many step-siblings, including Janka, Armin, Gábor, Ernő, Makor and Alexander. Alexander lived in Vrbova, owned a shoe shop and had two children: a daughter, Zelma, and a son, Walter. His family died in Auschwitz. Nothing is known about their lives. Since mandatory military service existed, he served his time in the Czech Army from 1924 to 1925. We have no details about his army service, only a picture of him in a

---

48 Alexander Goldstein, Chicago, email message to author, October 27, 2016.
49 SANR SA, f. OÚ SA 15568/1936, box n. 446.
50 SANR SA, f. OÚ SA 15568/1936, box n. 446.
51 SANR SA, f.NÚ Pered. 414/1937 box n. 30.

uniform. In 1927, Jakab bought and remodeled the house in which he had grown up as a child. His parents lived there with him.[52]

He married Berta Neuhauser on February 29, 1928. The marriage was arranged between them in Veľký Meder. She was born in Okoč and was four years older than him.[53] His mother, Magdalena, was not a pleasant mother-in-law. She and Berta had a very poor relationship. In their first year of marriage, Berta and Jakab gave birth to a daughter, Matilda (Hana); she was born on May 15, 1929. His grandfather, Leopold, died the same year and was buried in Galanta. On August 9, 1930, they had their second daughter, Vera (Ester). His mother continued to live with them until her death in 1938. Magdalena is buried in the Jewish cemetery in Pered, which became a memorial park in 1980.[54]

Jakab was taken to a Hungarian labor camp on April 1, 1943 and returned on May 1, 1945. Then he started a new life; on August 4, 1946 he married Erzsébet Löwinger (she was from Tomášikovo). They had one son together, Alexander. He was born in 1947 in Nové Zámky. Now he lives in Chicago. He still likes to visit Pered when he has the opportunity. He has not forgotten his roots.

After the war, Jakab continued working in his shop. He was very well known at this time. He was very helpful to customers. He extended the opening hours to serve the village's needs. In his shop, people could buy anything from sugar to a bicycle, so anything and everything. He lived near the Roman Catholic church. He lived an orthodox Jewish life. His wife tried to live according to Jewish customs.[55]

Jakab was very amiable. He lived among Pered's community. He had many friends. He liked smoking his cigars and loved playing cards. He spent lots of time with his friends (farmers, teachers, the Roman Catholic rector and so on), playing their favorite card games. He had a unique sense of humor and it was one of the reasons why he was very popular in the village.

---

52 Alexander Goldstein, Chicago, email message to author, November 3, 2016.
53 SANR SA, f. OÚ SA 148/1934, box n. 352.
54 Alexander Goldstein, Chicago, email message to author, November 5, 2016.
55 Alexander Goldstein, Chicago, email message to author, November 11, 2016.

During nationalization, his shop was nationalized and he became the store manager. But many witnesses remember that he had many certificates praising the good shop assistant or store manager in his shop. He was very capable at his job and he did it with love.

He died on June 16, 1979 at the hospital in Šaľa. He was buried according to Jewish tradition, in the Jewish cemetery in Galanta. In the village, his memory remains alive because everybody remembers that in Lebush's shop you could buy everything.

Church life in Pered

Church life developed hand in hand with cultural life and education was one of the vital parts of these lives. The Roman Catholic church was a typical church in Pered. Pered belonged to the Komárno diocese and the district of Šaľa. The church community became independent in 1805, until this year it had been a part of Žihárec's community.[56]

During the interwar period, Pered had its largest number of villagers. According to the census in 1930, the village had 3,946 Roman Catholic inhabitants, 130 Jewish people and 14 Protestants.[57]The Jewish community came from the orthodox branch; the branch base was in Galanta, where there was also the Rabbinate and registry office for Jewish people.

Olivér Ribány

"The writer and rector"

Olivér Ribány was born on December 18, 1848 in Trnava. His parents were József Ribány and Anna Vaczulík. He attended primary school in Trnava during 1853–1859, then studied at the gymnázium in Trnava in 1859–1867. After gaining his education from the gymnasium, he started to study theology in Ostrihom, were he graduated on July 10, 1868. On July 31, 1871 he was consecrated as a priest. After this event, he started his career in Neded as a temporary chaplain. He was there until October 1871, and later got a job as chaplain in Galanta, then in Trnava. From

---

56 SANR SA, f. OÚ SA 2771/1929, box n. 215.
57 *Encyklopédia židovských náboženských obcí.*, 195.

January 29, 1879, he was an administrator, later a priest in Ružindol. From there he was moved to Pered on September 13, 1907. There he remained until his death.

He was very wise and very good at languages. He could speak and write in Slovak, Hungarian, Latin, German, English, France and Italian. He was an able translator and did translations of literary works from French and German into Hungarian. He published his works in newspapers (Katolikus néplap, Magyar Sion, Magyar Korona). It is very interesting that he did not use his own name – he used pennames such as "Csákai Sándor", the initials "R.O." or "R. Olivér".[58]

He was the rector in Pered when on September 1, two church bells were withdrawn for military purposes.[59] He died at the age of 80 from a stroke on September 25, 1929. He was buried in Tešedíkovo.

Health service in the village

In the Austro-Hungarian Monarchy, the health service decreed by Law XIV of 1876 was a major problem. The health service, specifically medical practice, had been established according to Law XVIII of 1871. In this law, in § 74, it was written that a doctor must obtain his diploma at

---

58 *Magyar katolikus lexicon* accessed on September 23, 2016, http://lexikon. katolikus.hu/R/Rib%C3%A1ny.html

59 "On 1 September 1916 two bells from our church were taken. It was written about the first bell in Military Statement No. 311 that it weighed 285 kilograms. The patron saint of Hungary was seen on it and there was written: From churchgoers' collections in 1867, poured in Ferenc Walseras's workshop in Pest. On the second bell was written, according to Military Statement No. 312 that it weighed 93 kilograms, on the bell there was a picture of Christ on the Cross with the inscription: Sacred Heart have mercy on us. Queen of the Rosary intercede for us. It was poured by Frigyes Szeltenhoffer and his sons in Sopron, 1884. It was paid for by churchgoers from Pered. When the bells were removed, many churchgoers were near the church. When the bells were put on wagons, the believers decorated them with wreaths. The rector near to the cross in the entrance was standing delivering a speech. Churchgoers were crying. You could hear crying everywhere, everybody together started to sing a hymn and accompany the bells to the station. At the station an official obituary was written. At 11am the occasion ended." SANR SA. f. FÚ Pered. box n.11.

a university in the Austro-Hungarian Monarchy and had to have at least one year's practice.[60]

IgnácPollák
"The doctor"

Ignác Pollák was born in 1868 in Bratislava. His parents were Áron and Erzsébet Pollák. He obtained his medical diploma on June 24, 1894 in Vienna. Later he had vocational training at the Children's Dermatological Institute and public hospital in Vienna. He started to work in Pered as a general practitioner on January 1, 1897. As a state practitioner, he was registered in January 1924.[61] He worked as a general practitioner until his retirement. He was scheduled to retire on April 1, 1934. He did not serve as an ordinary soldier; he served as a doctor in his military service. First, he was in Žilina from July to August 1916.

Among the duties of the circuit doctors, many activities were listed such as checking meat or working as a coroner, but it was common that they had to operate and work as a dentist too. In his circuit there were Pered, Diakovce and Žihárec. He worked in Diakovce on the 3rd and 18th day of every month, and in Žihárec on the 5th and 20th days. Officially he worked in Pered, and in that village he had to secure his doctor's apartment. He had a small kitchen, room and storage room.[62]

---

60 According to § 142, Law XIV of 1876, every town or village which had more than 6,000 inhabitants needed to secure their own town or village doctors. Villages which had less than 6,000 inhabitants could join other villages' doctors' circuits. The village that wanted to be a seat of the circuit was elected by villages. If a village could not join other villages, their doctors' duties were performed by district doctors or the doctor from the hospital that was the nearest to this village. But the village needed to pay some money into the budget of the hospital. The village doctor was chosen by public tender (this was decreed in the law from 1871) and they were paid by the city or village council. According to this law, doctors had to treat their patients according to income. Poor people had to be treated for free and wealthier people had to pay according to their prescriptions. It was similar with vaccination.

61 SANR SA.f. OÚ SA, 2/1924 box n. 2.

62 SNA BA. f. The commission of health services, hereinafter f. PoZ. Dr. Pollák Ignác, box n. 309.

In 1896, he married his first wife Melánia Silberg; they had two daughters Aranka (July 12, 1898) and Šarolta (February 3, 1900). However, we do not know anything about them. His first wife died in 1925. He re-married on January 16, 1928; his wife was Janka Halami from Prešov.[63]

He was very good at languages and spoke Slovak, English and German fluently. We know from the documents that in 1934 he lived in Pered. He died at the age of 74 after heart problems in Bratislava and was buried in a Jewish cemetery in the city.[64] We assume he had moved there with his wife.

Feldmár Zoltán

"The friendly doctor"

He was born in Vlčany on November 16, 1906. His parents were Ernestína Spillman and Jakab Feldmár. His father was a trader. He was born one of twins; his brother Ferenc died in 1944. He was originally Jewish, but before his wedding with his wife in 1936, he converted to the Roman Catholic faith.[65]

After his elementary studies he started to study at Commenius University in Bratislava. He graduated on March 21, 1931 and passed his physical exams and did a course in social medicine in Prague. He attended military service in the divisional hospital in Plzeň in 1931 until September 1932. In December 1932, he was a secondary doctor in Ivančice, in Morava. After this, he became a circuit doctor in Pered.[66] During this, he married Cyprián Lelovics's daughter Zsófia. Their wedding was on July 12, 1936. In 1936, he converted from Judaism to the Roman Catholic faith. Maybe this was because his wife's family was devout believers. First, he was a circuit doctor from 1934 to 1938. On February 11, 1938, he became a circuit doctor in Pered.[67]

---

63 SNA BA. f. PoZ. Dr. Pollák Ignác, box n. 309.
64 Jewish cemetery. http://www.jewishcemetery.sk/fileadmin/book/#kniha-pochovaných/374-375. Accessed October 13, 2016.
65 SANR SA. f. OÚ SA. Withdrawing from the church. Dr. Zoltán Feldmár 1936, box n. 455.
66 SNA BA. f. PoZ. MUDr. Feldmár Zoltán, box n. 74.
67 SANR SA. f. OÚ SA, 1910/1938, box n. 252.

He had converted, but between 1943 and 1945, he did not get a job as a doctor because of racial reasons.[68] In the village, he had a surgery at his father-in-law's. In the 1950s, he had his own surgery in his house. His house was very modern. His wife was his nurse. They had three children: Zuzana (July 25, 1937), Ladislav (May 20, 1940) and Beatrix (September 22, 1943).

He was very good at languages, speaking Slovak, English and German fluently. He was a very capable doctor, and many witnesses remember that he would help with any problem. He performed operations in his surgery.

Later, they moved to Šaľa, where his wife was a nurse alongside the dentist Dr. Menzel. He worked in the hospital in Šaľa and Galanta for a long time. He passed away in 1971 and was buried in the cemetery in Šaľa. His wife died a very old lady, at the age of 96 in 2015.

Károly Thorma

"The first pharmacist"

He was born in 1873 in Izsák (Hungary); his parents were Ferenc Thorma and Judit Szalay. He established the first pharmacy in Pered in 1909, named "To the Guardian Angel".[69] In 1925, he moved to Pered together with his wife Dalmady Lenke.[70] He died on May 5, 1926. He was only 53 years old. He had heart problems. His wife, after his death, was the manager of their pharmacy. He was a very capable expert in pharmacy. People respected him. He was a very good friend of Mészáros Henrik and made a lot of medical preparations for him.

---

68 SANR SA, f. NÚ Pered, 4472/44, box n. 34
69 Katolikuslexikon, http://lexikon.katolikus.hu/G/gy%C3%B3gyszert%C3%A1r.
    html, accessed October 11, 2016,
70 SANR SA. f. NÚ Pered. Minutes of official Council 1919–1925, May 21, 1925.

Resumé

In today's world, interdisciplinary sciences are particularly well received. Although the social and human sciences have not lost their seriousness and importance, the 21st century brings much doubt to them. Technological modernization and advancement often shifts the subject of research out of their sights. It considers their research results to be unnecessary or impractical in this modern and busy world.

We cannot blame other sciences for the decline of the interest in history, ethnology, folklore and so on. Frequent reasons are unknown subjects and poor presentation of the results and objectives of their research.

A publication containing works of PhD students of the Department of Archeology, the Department of Ethnology and Folklore, the Department of History and the Department of Culture and Tourism Management of the Faculty of Arts at the University of Constantine the Philosopher in Nitra will dispel these doubts. It points out the importance of these sciences, and also takes many aspects of research into these sciences. It draws attention to many possibilities, whose variability and uniqueness, as well as the results of interdisciplinary research and other sciences are pushing humanity to modernize.

It is important to evaluate positively the possibility of presenting the results of the scientific work of the younger generation, publicly. Their collaboration reveals a lot of, not yet known research possibilities.

The presented paper is an excellent reflection bridge to other possibilities of scientific work. In addition to the presentation, its ambition is to help after a period of diminishing interest in re-starting scientific research in the humanities and social sciences.

List of Tables

References

Association of teachers from schools with regional education. *Združenie pedagógov zo škôl s regionálnou výchovou.* Accessed June 2, 2016. http://www.regioskola.sk/. Available on the internet: http://www. thefreedictionary.com/.

Bartko, Emil Tomáš. *Podoby slovenského tanečného umenia 1920–2010.* Vydanie prvé. Bratislava: Divadelný ústav. p. 259. 2011.

Bazovský, Igor. and Elschek, Kristián. *Osídlenie v Bratislave-Dúbravke v 9. -13. storočí II. Stredoveký dvorec.* In Zborník Slovenského národného múzea XCII. Archeológia 8. Bratislava, p. 85–96. 1998.

Bednárik, Rudolf. *Ľudovéstaviteľstvona Kysuciach.* Bratislava: Vydavateľstvo SAV, p. 248, 1968.

Belás, Ladislav. *Pôsobeniekysuckýchkňazov v pobočnomstánku Slovenského učenéhotovaryšstvavo Veľkom Rovom – Kysuckíkňazibe rnolákovci.* In Terra Kisucensis 1.Turzovka: TERRA KISUCENSIS, p. 99–104, 2008.

Belovič, Vladimír. *Hlavné dokumenty EÚ v oblasti vzdelávania.* In *Pedagogické rozhľady,* edited by Magazine methodological - teaching centers in Slovakia, 1–4. Banská Bystrica: MPC in Banská Bystrica, 2003.

Benža, Mojmír. *Martin Slivka.* In Botík, Ján – Slavkovský, Peter a kol. *Encyklopédia ľudovej kultúry Slovenska 2.* Bratislava: Veda, p. 152–153, 1995.

Beňko, Ján. *Osídlenie Kysúc.* In Správya informácie Kysuckéhomúzea 4/1980. Čadca: Kysuckémúzeum, p. 5–34, 1981.

Bešina, Daniel. *Zaniknutý románsky kostol sv. Martina na Baratke pri Leviciach, návrh na prezentáciu.* Nitra: Graduation theses, 2013.

Blaho, Ján. *Hlavné princípy a zásady scénického spracovania folklóru.* Rytmus. Bratislava: Obzor, 37(12), p. 17, 1986.

Blaho, Ján. *Premeny tanca – prenášanie tradičného ľudového tanca v súčasných podmienkach.* Rytmus. Bratislava: Obzor, 37(6), p. 10–11, 1986.

Blaho, Ján. *Scénické spracovanie ľudových tancov v amatérskych folklórnych súboroch – skúsenosti a úvahy choreografa.* Rytmus. Bratislava: Obzor, 37(7), p. 10–12, 1986.

162 References

Blaho, Ján. *Štylizácia a miera štylizácie folklóru*. Rytmus. Bratislava: Obzor, 37(9), p. 18–19, 1986.

Blaho, Ján. *Tradičné tance – základ práce amatérskych folklórnych súborov*. Rytmus. Bratislava: Obzor, 37(8), p. 14–15, 1986.

BÜCHLER, J. Róbert. *Encyklopédia židovských náboženských obcí*. SNM – múzeum židovskej kultúry. Edícia Judaica Slovaca. 3. 2012.

Carpenter, Mary W. *Health, Medicine, and Society in Victorian England*. London: Praeger, 2010.

Chotěbor, Petr and Smetánka, Zdeněk. *Panské dvory na české vesnici*. In Archaeologia historica 10, Brno: Department of Archaeology and Museology of the Faculty of Arts at Masaryk University, p. 47–56. 1985.

Cséfalvay, František et al. *Vojenské osobnosti dejín Slovenska 1939–1945*. Bratislava: Vojenský historický ústav, 2013.

Dorica, Jozef. *Rotunda sv.Juraja pri Nitrianskej Blatnici. Jej nové miesto medzi najstaršími sakrálnymi stavbami na Slovensku*. In Historická revue špeciál, Bratislava: Slovak Archeological and Historical Institute - SAHI, p. 62–67, 2013.

Dostál, Bořivoj. *Břeclav - Pohansko. Velkomoravský veľmožský dvorec IV*. Brno: University of J. E. Purkyně, 1975.

Drábová, Dominika. *Majer v Oščadnici v obdobírokov 1770–1850*. In TERRA KISUCENSIS VI, p. 75–84, 2015.

Dresler, Petr and Přichystalová, Renáta. *Břeclav - Pohansko. Veľkomoravské hradisko*. In Historická revue 12, Bratislava: Slovak Archeological and Historical Institute – SAHI, p. 45–50, 2014.

Dubská, Michala. *Kultúrne dedičstvo a kultúrny cestovný ruch*. Nitra: The Faculty of Art UKF in Nitra, 2015.

Duchovičová, Jana and Kurincová, Viera et al. *Teoretické základy výchovy a vzdelávania*. Nitra: Pedagogical faculty UKF in Nitra, 2012.

Dúžek, Stanislav. *Ide o tanečné súbory. Hudba, spev, tanec*. Bratislava: Obzor, 4(6), p. 179. 1976.

Fiala, Andrej and Habovštiak, Alojz and Štefanovičová, Tatiana. *Opevnené sídliská z 10. - 13. storočia na Slovensku*. In Archeologické rozhledy XXVII, Praha: Institute of Archeology of the CAS, p. 429–441, 1975.

Filip, Jan. *Keltové ve střední Evropě.* Praha: ČSAV, Monumentia archaeologica, 1956.

Grekov, Boris. *Kyjevská Rus.* Praha: Československá akademie věd, 1953.

Gažová, Viera. *Perspektívy kulturológie. Modely kultúrnej výchovy na prelome tisícročí.* In Acta Culturologica, edited by Viera Gažová, Bratislava: Department of culturology. The Faculty of Art UK in Bratislava, p. 202–218. 2003.

Habovštiak Alojz. *Stredoveká dedina na Slovensku.* Bratislava: Vydavateľstvo Obzor, 1985.

Habovštiak Alojz. *Stredoveké hrádky na Slovensku.* In Vlastivedný časopis 21, p. 2–8. 1972.

Hajko, Dalimír. *Globalizácia a kultúrna identita.* Nitra: Faculty of Art UKF in Nitra, 2005.

Hamar, Juraj. *Folklór v tieni scénického folklorizmu. Národopisná revue.* Na margo folklórneho hnutia na Slovensku po roku 1988. Strážnica: Národní ústav lidové kultury, 18(4), p. 215–255, 2008

Hejna, Antonín. *K situační a stavební formaci feudálního sídla v Evropě.* In Památky archeologické 56, Praha: Archeologický ústav AV ČR, p. 513–583. 1965.

Hejna, Antonín. *České tvrze.* Praha: Statní nakladatelství krásné literatury a umění, 1961.

Hensel, Witold. *Archeologia o początkach miast słowiańskich.* Wrocław - Warszawa – Kraków: Zakład Narodowy im. Ossolinskich, Wyd. PAN, 1963.

Herrnbrod, Adolf. *Stand der frühmittelalterlichen Mottenforschung im Rheinland.* In Château Gaillard 1, Caen: Etudes de castellologie européenne. I. Colloque des Andelys 30. Mai-4. Juni, p. 79–100. 1964.

Hinz, Herman. *Motte und donjon. Zur Frühgeschichte der mittelalterlichen Adelsburg.* Köln: Rheinland-Verlag, 1981.

Horváthová, Margaréta. *Nemci na Slovensku: Etnokultúrne tradície z aspektu osídlenia, remesiel a odievania.* Komárno: Fórum inštitút pre výskum menšín - Výskumné centrum európskej etnológie, 2002.

Hudecová, Antónia. *Formovaniežidovskej komunitynaKysuciach do konca 18. storočia.* In TERRA KISUCENSIS VI. Čadca: Kysuckátlačiar eňČadca, p. 59–73. 2015.

Jablonický, Jozef. *Povstanie bez legiend: dvadsať kapitol o príprave a začiatku Slovenského národného povstania.* Bratislava: Obzor, 1990.

Jankuhn, Herbert. *Die frühmittelalterliche Seehandelspätze im Nord- und Ostseeraum.* In Studien zu den Anfängen des europäischen Städtewesens, Vorträge und Forschungen IV. 1955.

Jaššo, Filip. *Stredoveké hrádky na západnom Slovensku.* In Proceedings of the Faculty of Arts UK, Bratislava: Charles University, p. 123–140. 2007.

Jelínková, Zdenka. *Veľa diskutujeme? Hudba, spev, tanec.* Bratislava: Obzor, 4(4), p. 118. 1966.

Johnová, Ratka. *Marketing kultúrniho dědičství a umění.* Praha: Grada, 2008.

Junas, Ján et al. *80 rokov Červeného kríža na Slovensku.* Bratislava: Finest, 1999.

Kaliský, Roman. *Folklór dnes. Kultúrny život.* Bratislava: Sväz československých spisovateľov, 13(19), p. 4. 1958.

Kamińska, Janina. *Grodziska stożkowate sladem posiadłości rycerskich XIII - XIV wieku.* In Prace i Materiały Muzeum Archeologicznego i Etnograficznego w Łódzi, Seria archeologiczna 13, Łódź: Museum of Archaeology and Ethnography in Łódź, p. 43–78. 1966.

Kašička, František. *Tvrze středních Čech.* Praha: Středisko Státní památkové péče a ochrany přírody středočeského kraje, 1984.

Kies, Walter. *Die Burgen in ihrer Funktion als Wohnbauten.* Studien zum Wohnbauten in Deutschland, Frankreich, England, und Italien von 11.bis 15. Jahrhundert. Munchen: Mikrokopie, 1961.

Konopáska, Martin. *Od tradícií k dnešku: 15 rokov súborov piesní a tancov. Ľudová tvorivosť.* Martin: Matica slovenská, 10(5), p. 209–213. 1960.

Kovačovič, Igor. *Ukážme si správnu cestu.Hudba, spev, tanec.* Bratislava: Obzor, 4(7), p. 210. 1966.

Koppány, Tibor. *XI. századi királyi udvarház maradványai Zircen.* In A Veszprém Megyei Múzeumok Közleményei 11, Veszprém, p. 139–147. 1972.

Kouřil, Pavel and Měřínský, Zdeněk and Plaček, Miroslav. *Opevněná sídla na Moravě a ve Slezku (vznik, vývoj, význam, funkce, současný stav a perspektivy dalšího výzkumu).* In Archaeologia historica 19,

Brno: Department of Archaeology and Museology of the Faculty of Arts at Masaryk University, p. 121–151. 1994.

Kováč, Dušan. *Kronika Slovenska 2. Slovensko v dvadsiatom storočí.* Praha: Fortuna Print & Adut, p. 608. 1999.

Kralovičová, Katarína. *Prehľad katolíckeho školstva na Kysuciach do I. pol. 20. storočia.* In TERRA KISUCENSIS 1/2008.Turzovka: TERRA KISUCENSIS, p. 167–189. 2008.

Kučera, Matúš. *Sociálna štruktúra obyvateľstva Slovenska v 10.-12. Storočí.* In Historický časopis 13, Bratislava: Historical Institute, p. 1–53. 1965

Kučera, Matúš. *Slovensko po páde Veľkej Moravy* Bratislava: VEDA Publisher Slovak Academy of Sciences, 1974.

Kyseľ, Vladimír. *Prehrávky folklórnych súborov.* Rytmus. Bratislava: Obzor, 30(11), p. 10–11. 1979.

Kyseľ, Vladimír. *Amatérske folklórne súbory v roku 1982.* Rytmus. Bratislava: Obzor, 33(12), p. 10–11. 1982.

Lacko, Martin. *Slovenské národné povstanie 1944.* Bratislava: Slovart, 2008.

Lauko, Viliam – Tolmáči, Ladislav. *Humánna geografia Slovenskej republiky. Dočasnéučebnétexty.* Bratislava: UK, p. 159. 2005.

Laš, Pavol. *Skalité, obec pod Trojačkom.* Skalité: ObecSkalité, p. 559. 2015.

Lenovský, Ladislav et al. *Cestovný ruch a kultúrne dedičstvo.* Nitra: The Faculty of Art UKF in Nitra, 2008.

Lenovský, Ladislav. *Kultúra kúpeľného mesta.* Nitra: The Faculty of Art UKF in Nitra, 2009.

Liščák, Marián. *Deti Bystríc*: Spoločensképomery v Starej a NovejBystrici i okolitýchdedinách v prvejpolovici 19. storočia. Krakow: SpolokSlovákov v Poľsku, p. 269. 2013.

Liščák, Marián. *Čadca v prvejpolovici 19.storočia.* In Kapitoly z dejínČadce: Odborný seminar pripríležitosti 480. Výročiazaloženiamesta. Čadca: Mesto Čadca a ŠA BY, pobočka Čadca, p. 35–51. 2014.

Liščák, Marián. *Z novýchvýskumov k dejinám Čadce v prvejpolovici 19.storočia.* In Človek, spoločnosť, doba. Stretnutiemladýchhistorikov III. Košice: Univerzita P. J. Šafárika v Košiciach, p. 116–127. 2014.

Marsina, Richard. *K staršímdejinám Kysúc.* In Správya informácieKysuck éhomúzea. 5–6 Čadca: Kysuckémúzeum, p. 61–80. 1983.

Michálek, Ján. *Za hlboké poznanie folklórnej tvorby nášho ľudu.* Kultúrny život. Bratislava: Sväz československých spisovateľov, 13(24), p. 6. 1958.

Mináč, Vladimír. *Tíha folklóru.* Literární noviny. Praha: Svaz československých spisovatelů, 7(12), p. 1. 1958.

Ministry of Culture of the Slovak Republic. *Declaration of NC SR on the Protection of Cultural Heritage in 2001.* Accessed October 12, 2016. http://old.culture.gov.sk/kulturne-dedicstvo/ochrana-pamiatok/vsledky/ deklaracia-o-ochrane-pamiatok.

Ministry of Culture of the Slovak Republic. *Development Strategy of Culture of the Slovak Republic for the years 2014–2020.* Accessed June 2, 2016. http://www.strategiakultury.sk/sites/default/files/STRATEGIA_ ROZVOJA_KULTURY_SR_NA_ROKY_2014-2020.pdf

Ministry of Education, Science, Research and Sport of the Slovak Republic. *Law no. 245/2008 Coll. on education and training (Education Law) and on amendment certain acts as amended.* Accessed October 12, 2016. https://www.minedu.sk/data/att/8206.pdf.

Ministry of Environment of the Slovak Republic. *National Strategy for Sustainable Development, Slovak Republic.* Accessed February 5, 2016.<http://www.minzp.sk/.../narodna-strategia-trvalo-udrzatelneho- rozvoja-slovenskej-republiky-cast-1.rtf>.

Mulík, Ján. *Dejiny kúpeľov a kúpeľníctva na Slovensku.* Bratislava: Osveta, 1981.

Müller, Róbert. *Karoling udvarház és temetője.* In Honfoglalás és régészet, Budapest: Balassi Kiadó, p. 91–98. 1994.

Müller-Wille, Michael. *Mittelalterliche Burghugel im nordlichen Rheinland.* Köln Graz: Böhlau Verlag, 1966.

Nekuda, Vladimír and Unger, Josef. *Hrádky a tvrze na Moravě.* Brno: Nakladatelství Blok v Brně 1981.

Nagy, Ludovicus. *Notitiae politico-geographico-statisticae inclyti regni Hungariae partiumqueeidemadnexarum.* Budae: Procusae Typis Annae Landerer, p. 640. 1828.

Nešporová, Tamara. *Výsledky historicko-archeologického výskumu na Trenčianskom hrade.* In Vlastivedný časopis 23, Bratislava, p. 142–143. 1974.

Novotný, Bohuslav. et al. *Encyklopédia archeológie.* Bratislava: Obzor, 1986.

Plaček, Miroslav. *Formy feudálního sídla moravského venkova.* In Archaeologia historica 24, Brno: Department of Archaeology and Museology of the Faculty of Arts at Masaryk University, p. 291–300. 1999.

Ondrejka, Kliment. *Nepomohla by tanečnej tvorbe väčšia nápaditosť?* Hudba, spev, tanec. Bratislava: Osveta, 2(9), p. 138. 1964.

Paráčová, Andrea. *Evanjelicke Kysuce a rekatolizacia.* In TERRA KISUCENSIS 1. Turzovka: TERRA KISUCENSIS, p. 37–50. 2008.

Paráčová, Andrea. *Panstvo Strečno (náčrtvzniku, vývoja a majetkovýchvzťahov).* In TERRA KISUCENSIS III. Turzovka: TERRA KISUCENSIS, p. 41–50. 2010.

Paráčová, Andrea. *Sporypanstiev Strečno a Budatín o hranicena Kysuciach.* In Zborník Kysuckéhomúzea 10, Čadca: Kysuckémúzeum, p. 29–36. 2006.

Paráčová, Andrea. *Z histórielesníctvana Kysuciach.* In Zborník Kysuckéhomúzea 9/2004. Čadca: Kysuckémúzeum, p. 25–40. 2004.

Plevza, Viliam. *Dejiny Slovenského národného povstania 1944. V. zväzok.* Bratislava: Pravda, 1984.

Podoláková, Ľubica. *Patronícia kysuckých chrámov a významné sakrálne pamiatky Kysúc.* In TERRA KISUCENSIS 1/2008. Turzovka, p. 105–122. 2008.

Polla, Belo and Slivka, Michal and Vallašek, Adrián. *K problematike výskumu hrádkov a hradov na Slovensku.* In Archaeologia Historica 6, Brno: Department of Archaeology and Museology of the Faculty of Arts at Masaryk University, p. 361–405. 1981.

Putz-Plecko, Barbara. Cultural education: *The promotion of cultural knowledge, creativity and intercultural understanding through education.* Vienna: University for Applied Arts, 2008. Accessed October 14, 2016. ww.dieangewandte.at/jart/prj3/.../EreportBparis0812.pdf.

Radig, Werner. *Die Siedlungstypen in Deutschland.* Berlin: Henschel, 1955.

Rahtz, Philip. *The Saxon and Medieval Palaces at Cheddar, Somerset.* In Medieval Archeology VI.–VII, p. 53–66. 1962.

Rebling, Eberhard. *Abeceda baletu (preklad vybraných kapitol).* Bratislava: VŠMU -Hudobno-tanečná fakulta, p. 64. 1986.

Rebro, Karol. *Urbárskaregulácia Márie Terézie a poddanskéúpravy Jozefa II. NaSlovensku.* Bratislava: SAV, p. 666. 1959.

Reinerth, Hans. *Vorgeschichte der deutschen Stämme.* Liepzig: Bibliographisches Institut, 1940.

Ruttkay, Alexander and Čaplovič, Dušan and Vallašek, Adrián. *Stredoveké feudálne sídla na Slovensku a ich hospodárske zázemie.* In Archaeologia historica 10, Brno: Department of Archaeology and Museology of the Faculty of Arts at Masaryk University, p. 241–254. 1985.

Ruttkay, Alexander and Ruttkay, Matej and Šalkovský, Peter. *Slovensko vo včasnom stredoveku.* Nitra: Archaeological Institute of the Slovak Academy of Science, 2002.

Ruttkay, Alexander. *Sídla spoločenských elít na strednom Ponitrí v 9. - 13. storočí.* In Dávne dejiny Nitry a okolia, Nitra: Archeologický Ustav SAV, p. 77–86. 2005.

Ruttkay, Alexander. *Výskum včasnostredovekého opevneného sídla v Ducovom, okres Trnava.* In Archeologické rozhledy XXIV, Praha: Academia Praha, p. 130–139. 1972.

Ruttkay, Alexander. *Včasnostredoveký sídliskový komplex a Rotunda sv. Juraja pri Nitrianskej Blatnici.* In Historická revue špeciál 2013, Bratislava: Slovak Archaeological and Historical Institute - SAHI, p. 55–61, 2013.

Ruttkay, Alexander. *Správa o výskume v Nitrianskej Blatnici v roku 1980.* Research report. AVANS, Nitra, p. 256–258. 1980.

Ruttkay, Matej. *Príspevok k poznaniu malých stredovekých opevnení na juhozápadnom Slovensku.* In Archaelogia historica 17, Brno: Department of Archaeology and Museology of the Faculty of Arts at Masaryk University, p. 253–261. 1992.

Rychlík, Jan. *Češi a Slováci ve 20.století: Česko-slovenské vztahy 1914–1945. Zväzok 1.* Praha: Vyšehrad, 1997.

Secondary Vocational School of Hotel Services and Business Nové Zámky. *The school educational program Hotel Academy for the Study Field 6323 6.* Accessed March 3, 2015. http://www.hosnz.sk/wp-content/uploads/03-SkVP-2013-HOTELOVA-AKADEMIA-aktualizovany-20151.pdf>.

Schadn, P. Hans. *Die Hausberge und verwandten Wehranlagen in Niederösterreich: ein Beitrag zur Geschichte des mittelalterlichen Befestigungswesens und seiner Entwicklung vom Ringwall bis zur*

Mauerburg und Stadtumwehrung In Prähistorische Forschungen 3, Wien: F. Berger, p. 512. 1953.

Shay, Anthony. *Choreographic Politics. State Folk Dance Companies, Representation, and Power.* Middletown, Connecticut: Wesleyan University Press, p. 249. 2002.

Schlag, Gottfried. *Die deutschen Kaiserpfalzen.* Frankfurt: Klostermann, 1940.

Slivka, Martin. *K dejinám scénických foriem folklóru I.* Rytmus. Bratislava: Obzor, 27(9), p. 11. ISSN 0231-7214. 1976.

Sokolovič, Peter. *Perzekúcie na Slovensku v rokoch 1938–1945.Zväzok 7.* Bratislava: Ústav pamäti národa, 2008.

State Vocational Training Institute. *Methodology for creation of school educational programs.* Accessed February 17, 2015. http://www.siov.sk/index/open_file.php?ext_dok=10882.

State Vocational Training Institute. *The national education program for vocational education and training group of studying and training branches 62 economics 63.64 Economics and Organisation, Retail and Services I., II.*Accessed March 20, 2016. http://www.siov.sk/statne-vzdelavacie-programy/9411s.

Szeghalmy, Gyula. *Felvidék.* Budapest: Városok Monográfiája kiadó hivatala, p. 257. 1940.

Szőke, Miklós Béla. *Pannónia a Karoling-korban.* In Akadémiai doktori értekezés tézisei, Budapest 2011. http://real-d.mtak.hu/541/1/dc_205_11_tezisek.pdf

Šalkovský, Peter. *K problematike opevnených sídiel vo včasnom stredoveku na Slovensku.* In Acta Historica Neosoliensia 15, Banská Bystrica: Department of History, Faculty of Humanities in Banská Bystrica, p. 47–60. 2012.

Štefanovičová, Tatiana. *Blatnohrad. Osudy Pribinu a Koceľa po opustení Nitrianska.* In Historická revue 12, Bratislava: Slovak Archaeological and Historical Institute - SAHI, p. 72–76. 2014.

Švehlák, Svetozár. *Sociálne a kultúrno-historické korene súčasného folklorizmu.* In Folklór a umenie dneška (k štúdiu folklorizmu v súčasnej kultúre). Bratislava: Osvetový ústav, p. 20–32. 1980.

The Education, Audiovisual and Culture Executive Agency. *Arts and Cultural Education at School in Europe.* Accessed March 3, 2016.

http://eacea.ec.europa.eu/education/eurydice./documents/thematic_
reports/113SK.pdf

The University Library in Bratislava. *Convention for the Protection of the World Cultural and Natural Heritage.* Accessed January 28, 2016. http://www.ulib.sk/sk/strediskounesco/svetove-dedicstvo/dohovor-ochrane-svetoveho-kulturneho-prirodneho-dedicstva/.

Timpel, Wolfgang. *Gommerstedt bei Bösleben, Kr. Arnstadt. Burghügel und Siedlung des Mittelalters.* In Ausgrabungen und Funde Bd. 21, p. 142–143. 1976.

Treťjakov, Pavel Michajlovič. *U kolébky staré rusy.* Praha: Státní nakladatelství politické literatury Praha 1958.

Turek, Ivan. *Didaktika.* Bratislava: edícia ŠKOLA Wolters Kluwer, 2014.

Unger, Josef. *Zpevňování svahů u opevněných objektů jižní Moravy 13.století.* In Archaeologica Historica 8, Brno: Department of Archaeology and Museology of the Faculty of Arts at Masaryk University, p. 521–528. 1983.

Urbarium of Budatín from 1658. In Marsina, Richard – Kušík, Michal. UrbárefeudálnychpanstievnaSlovensku II. Bratislava: Vydavateľstvo SAV, p. 280–306. 1959.

Uslar, Rafael. *Studien zu frühgeschichtlichen Befestigungen zwischen Nordsee und Alpen.* Köln-Graz: Bohlau Verlag 1964.

Vecco, Marilena. *A definition of cultural heritage: From the tangible to the intangible.* In Journal of Cultural Heritage. 11(3), July–September, p. 321–324. 2010.

Velička, Drahomír. *Dejinyfarnosti do roku 1918.* In Vysokánad Kysucou. Turany: obec Vysoká nad Kysucou, p. 71–97. 2014.

Velička, Drahomír. *Oščadnica.* In Osídlenie Kysúc. Dissertation Thesis. Trnava: Faculty of Arts Trnava University in Trnava, p. 166–170. 2009.

Velička, Drahomír. *OtázkazaloženiakatolíckychfarnostínahornýchK ysuciach v 17. a v I. polovici 18.storočia.* In TERRA KISUCENSIS 1.Turzovka: TERRA KISUCENSIS, p. 59–78. 2008.

Velička, Drahomír. *Zaniknutédrevenékostoly v kysuckomPobeskydí II.* In Práce a studiumuzea Beskyd. Frýdek-Místek, 22, p. 7–26. 2010.

Zatloukalová, Andrea. *Poddanské dediny mesta Žiliny (Závodie, Krásno nad Kysucou, Horelica, Oščadnica, Zborov).* In Vlastivednýzborník Považia XXI. Žilina: Považské múzeum, p. 151–165. 2002.

Zálešák, Cyril. *Propagujeme nové metódy práce v súboroch ľudového tanca.* Ľudová tvorivosť. 2(1–2), Martin: Matica slovenská, p. 40–41. 1953.

Zálešák, Cyril. *Problémy tanečného umenia.* Hudba, spev, tanec. Bratislava: Osveta, 2(3), p. 35–36. 1964.

Zálešák, Cyril. *Ideme správnym smerom?* Hudba, spev, tanec. Bratislava: Obzor, 3(3). s. 59–61. ISSN 0441-3873. 1965.

Zálešák, Cyril. *Ideme správnou cestou?* Hudba, spev, tanec. Bratislava: Obzor, 3(4), p. 85–86. 1965.

Zálešák, Cyril. *Roztancovaná zem.* Hudba, spev, tanec. Ideový a umelecký vývin súborov. Bratislava: Obzor, 6(12), p. 361–363. 1968.

Zálešák, Cyril. *Folklórne hnutie na Slovensku.* Vydanie prvé. Bratislava: Obzor, p. 312. 1982.

Zima, Štefan. *Usmerňovať prácu folklórnych súborov.* Rytmus. Bratislava: Obzor, 31(4), p. 10–11. 1980.

Archive sources:

Archive of the Ministry of Interior of SR – Military historical archive, *Profesionálne a sociálne skupiny v SNP*, file Živena, BURAJOVÁ, Ľudmila et al. Životopisy žien – Účastníčok SNP, p. 139.

CALENDARIUM DIOECESANUM CLERI NITRIENSIS AD ANNUM JESU CHRISTI 1790, 1796, 1797, 1800, 1805–1816. (16 volumes).

SCHEMATISMUS VENERABILIS CLERI DIOECESIS NITRIENSIS PRO ANNO A CHRISTO NATO 1819–1922. (114 volumes).

Slovak National Archive in Bratislava

Fond The Commission of Education.

Fond The Commission of health services.

State Archive in Nitra, Šaľa department

Fond District in Šaľa (1922–1938).

Fond Main Service Office in Šaľa.

Fond Notary Office in Pered.

Fond Parochial Office in Tešedíkovo.

Fond Personal fund of the Meszáros-Lelovics family.

Maps

Basic map of Čadca district 1: 50 000. Harmanec: Úradgeodézie, kartografie a katastra Slovenskej republiky.

Azelsőkatonaifelméres. DVD Arcanum, Budapest, 2002.

Austrian State Archive/Military Archive, Vienna (ŐsterreichichesStaatsarc hiv), Second Military Survey Section No. 31–32, 31–33.

Internet sources

http://lexikon.katolikus.hu/.

http://www.jewishcemetery.sk/

Information

Alexander Goldstein, Chicago, email message to author, October–November 2016.

Beáta Kopáčiková, Malinovo, email message to author, September 2015.

Gyula Varga, Tešedíkovo. According to a conversation with the author, October 2016.

Jozef Dráb *1967.

Juraj Lelovics, Šaľa. According to a conversation with the author, October 2016.

Milan Hvižďák, choreographer, *1937.

Igor Kovačovič, choreographer, *1938.

Vladimír Urban, choreographer, *1946.

Other sources

Chronicle of the Hungarian Language Elementary School in Tešedíkovo (1925–1941). Jozef Darázss's transcription.

Chronicle of the village Pered No. 2 (1975–1978).

Kasuba, István. *Csorvási Arcok 15. Mészáros Henrik. Csorvási Hírádó*, September 4, 1999.

Warsaw Studies in Philosophy and Social Sciences

Edited by Tadeusz Szawiel and Jakub Kloc-Konkołowicz

www.peterlang.com